Kakuro
FOR
DUMMIES®

by Andrew Heron

JOHN WILEY & SONS, LTD

Kakuro For Dummies®
Published by
John Wiley & Sons, Ltd
The Atrium
Southern Gate
Chichester
West Sussex
PO19 8SQ
England

E-mail (for orders and customer service enquires): cs-books@wiley.co.uk

Visit our Home Page on www.wileyeurope.com

Copyright © 2005 Crosswords Ltd

Published by John Wiley & Sons, Ltd, Chichester, West Sussex

For general information on our other products and services, please contact our Customer Care Department within the U.S. at 800-762-2974, outside the U.S. at 317-572-3993, or fax 317-572-4002.

For technical support, please visit www.wiley.com/techsupport.

Wiley also publishes its books in a variety of electronic formats. Some content that appears in print may not be available in electronic books.

British Library Cataloguing in Publication Data: A catalogue record for this book is available from the British Library

ISBN-13: 978-0-470-02822-3
ISBN-10: 0-470-02822-X

Printed and bound in Great Britain by Clays

10 9 8 7 6 5 4 3 2 1

Contents at a Glance

Publisher's Acknowledgments

We're proud of this book; please send us your comments through our Dummies
online registration form located at www.dummies.com/register/.

Some of the people who helped bring this book to market include the following:

Acquisitions, Editorial, and Media Development

Executive Project Editor: Martin Tribe

Development Editor: Daniel Mersey

Executive Editor: Jason Dunne

Commissioning Editor: Alison Yates

Cartoons: Rich Tennant
(www.the5thwave.com)

Composition Services

Project Coordinator: Kristie Rees

Layout and Graphics: Karl Brandt,
Jonelle Burns, Denny Hager,
Shelley Norris, Heather Ryan,
Rashell Smith

Proofreaders: Brian H. Walls

Special Help: Rev Mengle

Publishing and Editorial for Consumer Dummies

Diane Graves Steele, Vice President and Publisher, Consumer Dummies

Joyce Pepple, Acquisitions Director, Consumer Dummies

Kristin A. Cocks, Product Development Director, Consumer Dummies

Michael Spring, Vice President and Publisher, Travel

Kelly Regan, Editorial Director, Travel

Publishing for Technology Dummies

Andy Cummings, Vice President and Publisher, Dummies Technology/
General User

Composition Services

Gerry Fahey, Vice President of Production Services

Debbie Stailey, Director of Composition Services

Introduction

● ●

*T*he Japanese puzzlers who popularized sudoku and brought it to millions of solvers around the world have done it again with kakuro. What is even more amazing is that the route taken from relative obscurity to stardom is exactly the same journey that sudoku took.

Kakuro – the New Sudoku

Those of you who come to kakuro from sudoku-solving are at something of an advantage. Much of the logic and some of the terminology are similar. However, one very big difference exists between the two puzzles – sudoku is solved with logic alone, but kakuro requires some additional numeracy skills. You also need to know about candidates – a collection of digits that might possibly be the number for any one square (don't worry, I explain these in Chapter 1).

About This Book

Whether you've picked up this book wondering what the whole kakuro thing is about, are just starting on your first kakuro puzzles, or have been ferreting away through a whole host of them as quickly as possible, this book is for you.

I've included some invaluable hints on the strategy of the game as well as 240 puzzles of varying degrees of difficulty – and their answers, of course. To give you the best grounding in the rules and strategy of kakuro, I've included a few icons to help you navigate your way through the text:

This icon targets hints and shortcuts to solving kakuro puzzles.

Take these important points into account when working your way through a kakuro puzzle.

Where you see this icon, you'll find information on the technical side of the game. You can skip these bits if you want.

If you're already an old hand at kakuro, head straight through to Part II to start solving puzzles. If you're new to kakuro, pick up my hints and tips on mastering the game first by heading to Part I. Part III contains answers to the puzzles, but you wouldn't cheat by looking there first, would you?

The rise of kakuro

Just as sudoku was taken up by a Japanese publisher to become a favourite with that country's puzzlers, so too was kakuro. Its final steps into the limelight were taken in the same way as sudoku had gained its massive popularity – through the British national newspapers.

Part I

Getting to Know Kakuro

I'm mathematically dyslexic. But it's not unusual — 100 out of every 15 are. And it doesn't stop me from doing Kakuro.

In this part . . .

Whether you're new to kakuro or an experienced puzzle solver, understanding the strategy behind the game can only improve your solving skills. I cover the basics of kakuro and give you tips on approaching the puzzles methodically.

Chapter 1

Understanding Kakuro

Kakuro puzzles may look familiar, and they may look easy, but don't be fooled. While the elements that you use to solve the puzzles are simple numbers, how you go about using them can be a bit tricky. This chapter covers a few of the kakuro-solving ground rules, giving you all the strategy tools you need.

The Aim of Kakuro

A kakuro puzzle looks a lot like a crossword puzzle, with interlocking horizontal rows and vertical columns of squares (called *blocks*). Like a crossword, if a square is in both a row and a column, the character for that square must work for both the row and the column. But there the similarity ends, because all the characters that you put in the individual squares are numbers.

The original U.S. title of the puzzle – 'Cross Sums' – hints at the nature of kakuro. In the black squares around the edges of the blocks are numbers, called *clues*. These clues tell you the sum of the numbers in that block. In other words, if the clue is a 9, the correct answers to the individual squares in that block will add up to 9. *Across clues* are represented by the numbers printed on the black squares above the diagonal line and *down clues* are those below the line.

Kakuro has only one other trivial little rule to puzzle puzzlers: You cannot repeat any number in a given block. When you've correctly filled in every square so that the numbers in all the blocks equal their clues without repeating numbers in any block, you've completed the puzzle. Figure 1-1 shows a completed kakuro puzzle.

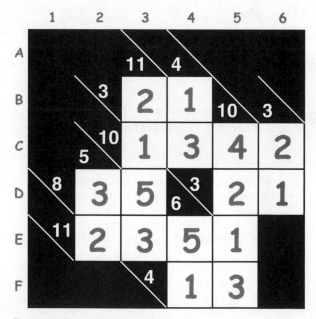

Figure 1-1: A completed kakuro puzzle.

Solving a Kakuro

Those blocks don't fill themselves in, you know. So this section presents you with the basic tools you need to tackle your first kakuro puzzles.

Understanding the clues

So how do you know which number goes where in a given kakuro puzzle? By following the clues on the grid.

As an example, say the clue is 3. This clue has two empty squares adjacent to it that make up the block. The only possible solution to a 3 in two squares is 1 and 2 (1 + 2 = 3). Similarly the solution to 4 in two squares is 1 and 3 (1 + 3 = 4). This can be the *only* solution to 4 because 2 + 2 would break the rule of no number being repeated in any block. Simple!

I mentioned *4 in two* in the previous paragraph. That's the way I'll express the clues from here on, so when you see *38 in six* you'll know that I mean 38 (the clue) has a block of six digits as its solution.

Getting down to basics

Two types of calculations help you through the world of kakuro:

- Combinations
- Fixed values

The following sections explain what you need to know about each to solve a kakuro.

Working out combinations

The numbers that you place in the boxes of a given block are called *combinations*. Two combinations are shown in the preceding section 'Understanding the clues': 1 and 2 making 3, and 1 and 3 making 4. Another example might be 10 in three, where the combination is 1, 2, and 7.

Some combinations (3 in two and 4 in two, for example) are sums that can only be worked out with specific numbers. For example, 3 in two can only be accomplished using 1 and 2, while 4 in two can only be 1 and 3. No other combinations work for these numbers without breaking the rule of not repeating digits. If a block has a clue that can only be solved with one combination of numbers (such as 3 in two and 4 in two), those combinations are referred to as *known combinations*.

Clues that have known combinations are extremely useful, so useful that I've provided you with a chart of them in Figure 1-9 (near the end of this chapter).

'Very interesting', you might say, 'but how does that help me solve kakuro?' Well, if two known combinations cross one another and they share only one digit, the square where they coincide must be the value of that digit. Say, for example, a 4 in two (1, 3) crosses a 38 in six (3, 5, 6, 7, 8, 9). The square where they cross must have the value of 3, because that's the only digit that they share. However, if the 4 in two crosses a 6 in three (1, 2, 3), the square in common could be either a 1 or a 3.

You can sometimes use this same principle for blocks that involve numbers without known combinations. Even if you can't come up with the final value for a square, you can at least narrow the possible candidates. For example, if you have a 10 in three, which is not a known combination, the candidate numbers for the three squares would be some combination involving 1, 2, 3, 5, 6, or 7. If a 3 in two crosses that 10 in three, the only candidates possible for the square where the two blocks coincide are the 1 and 2.

Candidates are the possible number choices you can insert into any square.

Figuring out fixed values

Another important concept is the *fixed value*. This is where a square's value is locked by the rules of kakuro – essentially, knowing what a square's value is by knowing all of the other numbers which it can't be.

Think of this as the process of elimination. For example, if the clue calls for the known combination of 7 in three – a known combination involving a 1, 2, and a 4 – and you've already got the 1 and the 2 accounted for, you know the remaining square must have a value of 4.

Working through Your First Kakuro

Take a look at a simple kakuro puzzle at Figure 1-2. They don't come much simpler than this, but it serves to illustrate all the points discussed in this chapter. For the purposes of explanation, I've numbered the grid: rows are A–F and columns 1–6.

Working through known combinations

Known combinations are so important that you should look for them first. The process of entering the candidates from any known combinations allows you to narrow down your choices and solve any easy clues straight away.

Figure 1-2: Your puzzle awaits. Tempted?

The example puzzle in Figure 1-2 has a load of known combinations: a bunch of 3s and 4s in two and a couple of 10s and 11s in four. Entering all the candidate numbers for these squares leaves just one completely unknown number in square D2, but stick with the known combinations first before looking at that one!

Looking at all the known combinations, only one square exists where you can make use of the rule about single common numbers: B4, where 4 in two and 3 in two both uniquely share the number 1. I've filled this – along with all the candidates – in on Figure 1-3. First number solved.

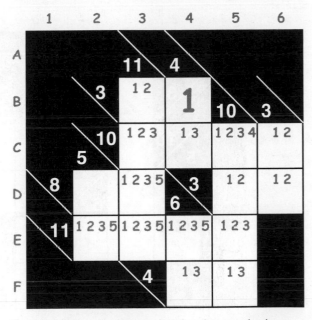

Figure 1-3: The candidates are placed, and one number is already solved.

Now look at F4. This square helps demonstrate the concept of fixed values. The candidates for F4 must be 1 and 3, the only two numbers that work for 4. But look at the down clue that coincides with this square, a 6 in two. If you used a 3 in square F4, then to add up to six you'd have to use another 3 in square E4, which would mean two 3s in the block, and that isn't allowed. So because you can't repeat numbers, the value at F4 can't be a 3, so it must be a 1. And that means that E4 must be a 5 and F5 must be a 3; and as you have the 1 in B4, then B3 must be a 2 and C4 must be a 3. Great! That's five more squares solved, as shown in Figure 1-4.

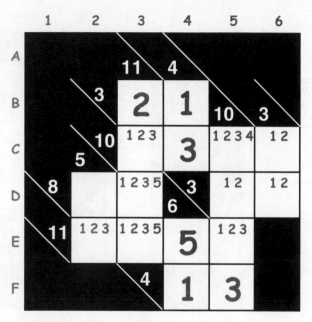

Figure 1-4: Fixed values help solve a few more squares.

Reducing candidates

Now that some numbers have been solved, use the rule of non-repetition to reduce the options for candidates in unsolved squares. For example, as column 5 already has a 3, no other square in column 5 can be a three. That means your options look like like Figure 1-5.

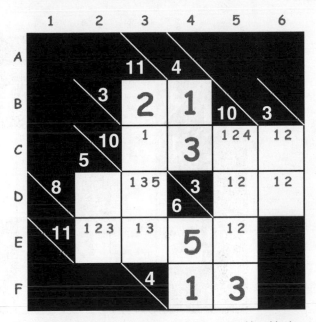

Figure 1-5: Knowing that numbers can't be repeated in a block narrows down your choice of candidates.

You've probably noticed that the process of reducing candidates revealed some more solved squares: at C3 the only candidate left is a 1, so that has to be the solution for that square. That reduces the options at D3 and E3, leaving only a 3 at E3, therefore resolving the square at D3 to 5. Also, a lone 4 is at C5 – if it doesn't appear anywhere else in either of the blocks that coincide at C5, then that has to be the number for that square. That's the state of play recorded in Figure 1-6.

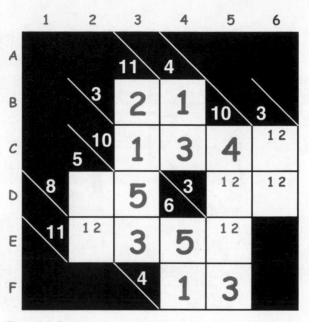

Figure 1-6: Reducing the candidates solves a few more squares.

Back to reducing candidates. At row C, you've already solved the 1 at C3, so the 1 at C6 can go, leaving the 2 at that square. This solves the square at D6, which in turn solves D5 and E5, as shown in Figure 1-7.

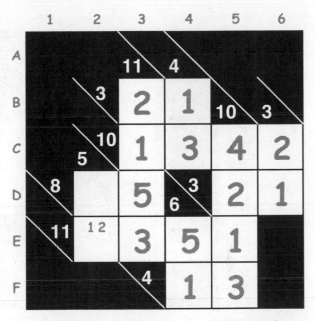

Figure 1-7: Filling in squares reduces other candidates and solves more blocks.

Now you're on the last lap. The square at E2 can only be a 2, as there is already a 1 in row E. And if E2 is a 2 then D2 must be a 3 to give a sum of 5 for that block. The 3 at D2 is proved by the 8 in two at D1, and Figure 1-8 shows you the way home.

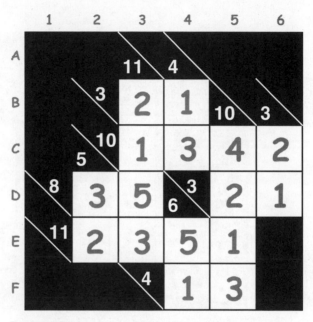

Figure 1-8: All done! Using a little skill and logic, the puzzle is solved.

Would that all kakuro were that simple, but this puzzle should serve to encourage you to make a start with confidence. Figure 1-9 shows known combinations to help you out. This chart may look daunting, but, as you practice kakuro, the numbers stick in your mind, and in no time at all you'll have no need to keep referring to it. I can almost guarantee that you've remembered the combinations for 3, 4, 10 and 11 already.

Clue	Cells	Combination
3	2	1, 2
4	2	1, 3
16	2	7, 9
17	2	8, 9
6	3	1, 2, 3
7	3	1, 2, 4
23	3	6, 8, 9
24	3	7, 8, 9
10	4	1, 2, 3, 4
11	4	1, 2, 3, 5
29	4	5, 7, 8, 9
30	4	6, 7, 8, 9
15	5	1, 2, 3, 4, 5
16	5	1, 2, 3, 4, 6
34	5	4, 6, 7, 8, 9
35	5	5, 6, 7, 8, 9
21	6	1, 2, 3, 4, 5, 6
22	6	1, 2, 3, 4, 5, 7
38	6	3, 5, 6, 7, 8, 9
39	6	4, 5, 6, 7, 8, 9
28	7	1, 2, 3, 4, 5, 6, 7
29	7	1, 2, 3, 4, 5, 6, 8
41	7	2, 4, 5, 6, 7, 8, 9
42	7	3, 4, 5, 6, 7, 8, 9
Any	8	1 to 9 (except 45 − clue)
Any	9	All of 1 to 9

Figure 1-9: Known combinations help you solve kakuro puzzles. Keep this handy!

Part II
Kakuro Puzzlemania

The 5th Wave   By Rich Tennant

"The divorce was amicable. She got the Jetta, the sailboat and the recumbent bike. I got the Kakuro books."

In this part . . .

*L*ooking for some puzzle-solving fun? Well, this is the Part for you. I've included 240 puzzles of increasing difficulty to try your hand at. Start with the first one to ease yourself in, or jump in at the (deep) end if you're feeling confident about your kakuro solving skills. Either way I hope you enjoy solving the puzzles as much as I have enjoyed compiling them.

Easy Does It

Puzzle 1: Easy

Puzzle 2: Easy

Puzzle 3: Easy

Puzzle 4: Easy

Puzzle 5: Easy

Puzzle 6: Easy

Puzzle 7: Easy

Puzzle 8: Easy

Puzzle 9: Easy

Puzzle 10: Easy

Puzzle 11: Easy

Puzzle 12: Easy

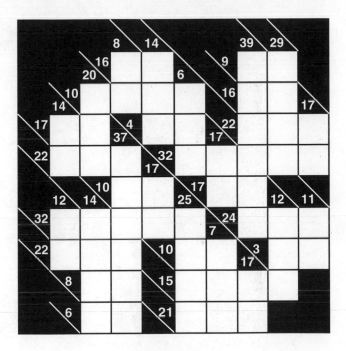

Puzzle 13: Easy

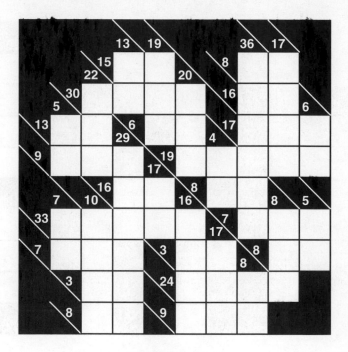

Puzzle 14: Easy

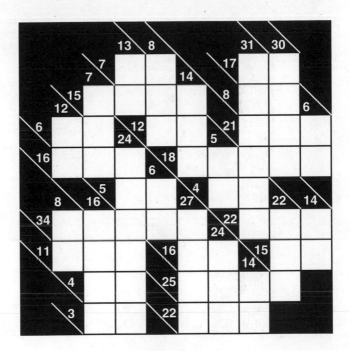

Puzzle 15: Easy

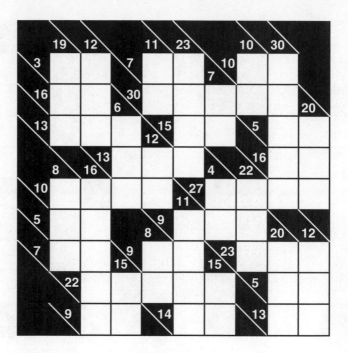

Puzzle 16: Easy

Puzzle 17: Easy

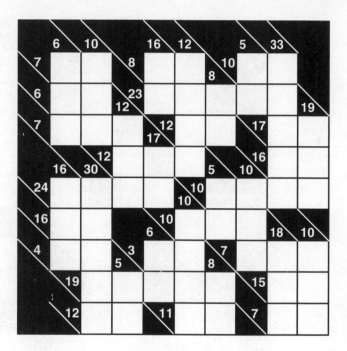

Puzzle 18: Easy

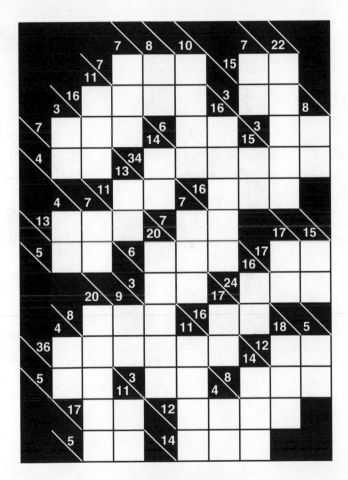

Puzzle 19: Easy

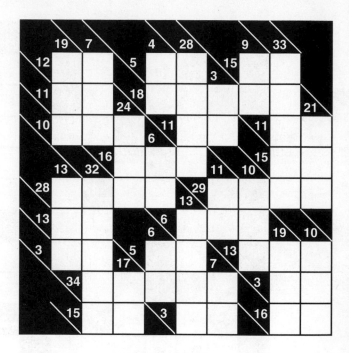

Puzzle 20: Easy

Puzzle 21: Easy

Puzzle 22: Easy

Puzzle 23: Easy

Puzzle 24: Easy

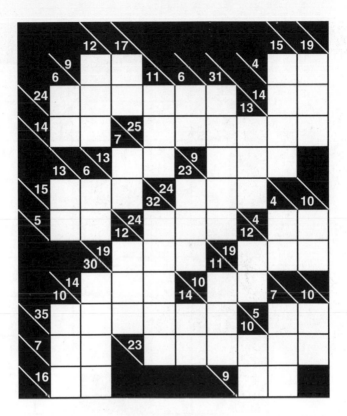

Puzzle 25: Easy

Puzzle 26: Easy

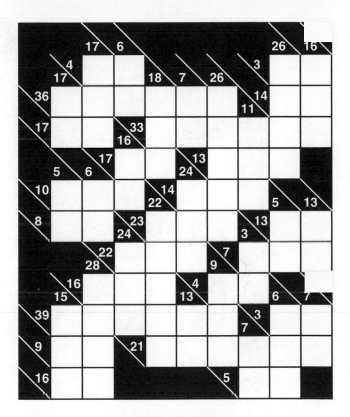

Puzzle 27: Easy

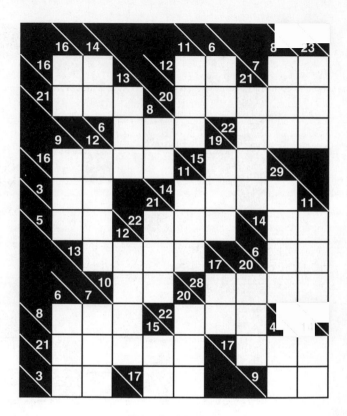

Puzzle 28: Easy

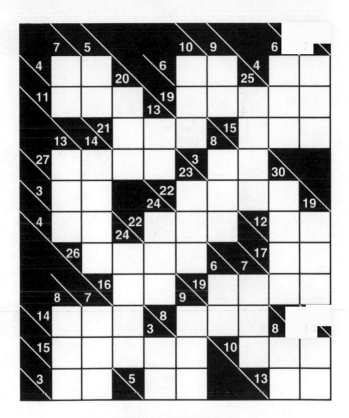

Puzzle 29: Easy

Puzzle 30: Easy

Puzzle 31: Easy

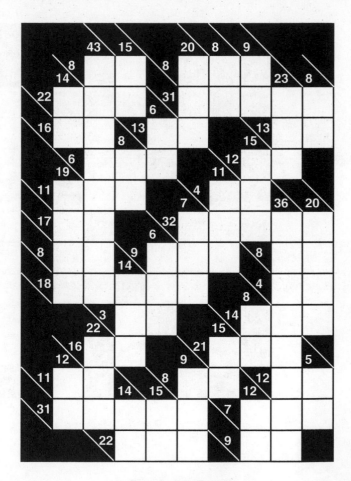

Puzzle 32: Easy

Puzzle 33: Easy

Puzzle 34: Easy

Puzzle 35: Easy

Puzzle 36: Easy

Puzzle 37: Easy

Puzzle 38: Easy

Puzzle 39: Easy

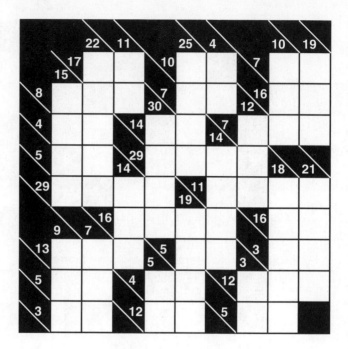

Puzzle 40: Easy

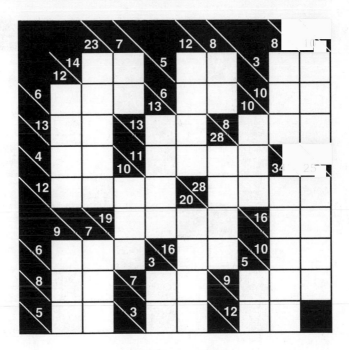

Puzzle 41: Easy

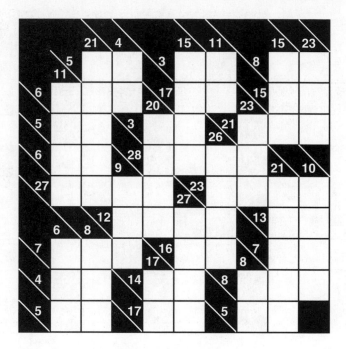

Puzzle 42: Easy

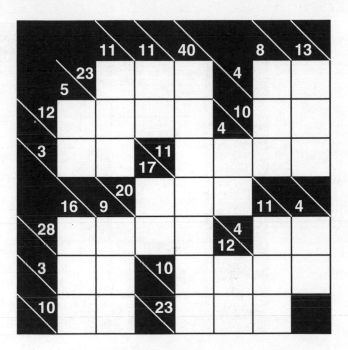

Puzzle 43: Easy

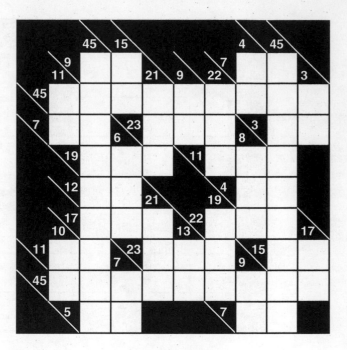

Puzzle 44: Easy

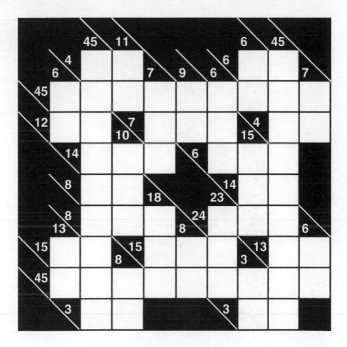

Puzzle 45: Easy

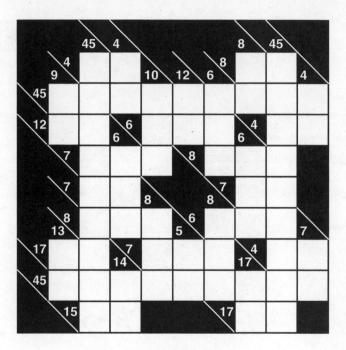

Puzzle 46: Easy

Puzzle 47: Easy

Puzzle 48: Easy

Puzzle 49: Easy

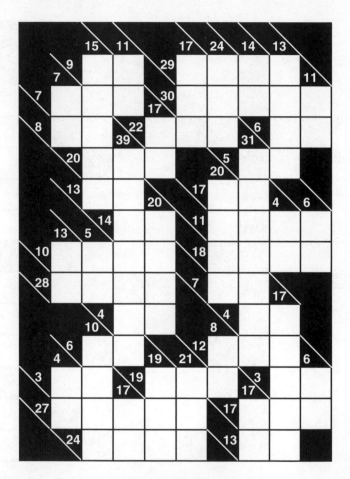

Puzzle 50: Easy

Puzzle 51: Easy

Puzzle 52: Easy

Puzzle 53: Easy

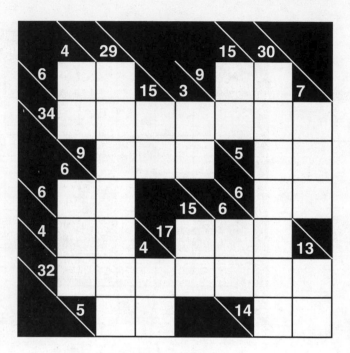

Puzzle 54: Easy

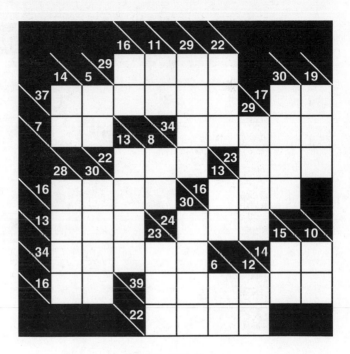

Puzzle 55: Easy

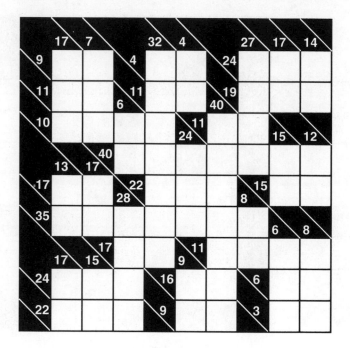

Puzzle 56: Easy

Puzzle 57: Easy

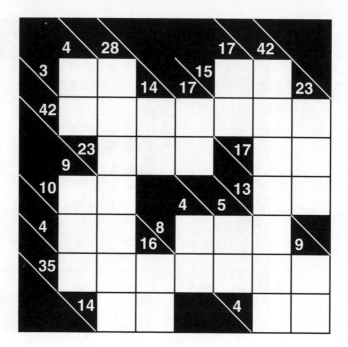

Puzzle 58: Easy

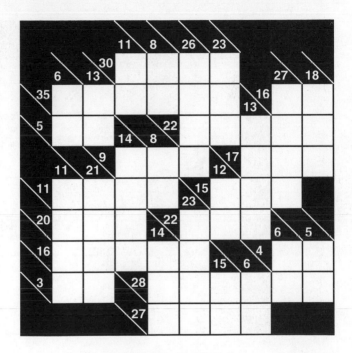

Puzzle 59: Easy

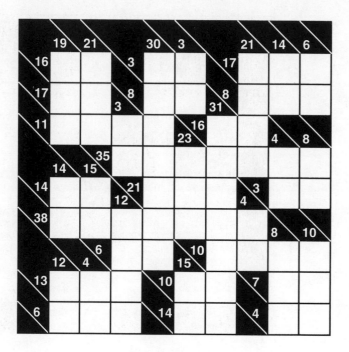

Puzzle 60: Easy

Puzzle 61: Easy

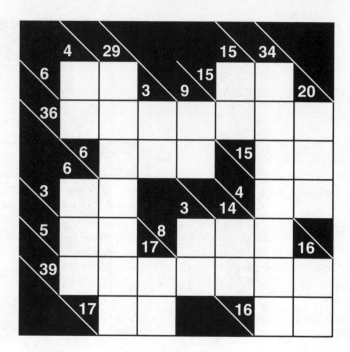

Puzzle 62: Easy

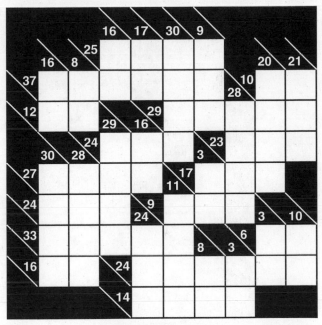

Puzzle 63: Easy

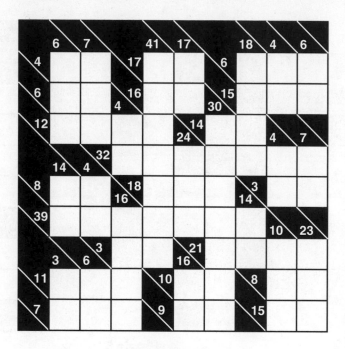

Puzzle 64: Easy

Puzzle 65: Easy

Puzzle 66: Easy

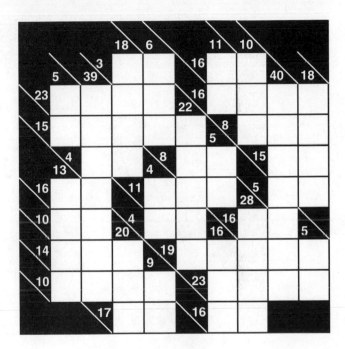

Puzzle 67: Easy

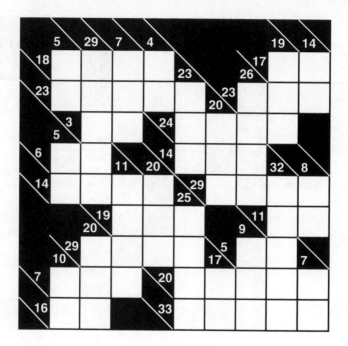

Puzzle 68: Easy

Puzzle 69: Easy

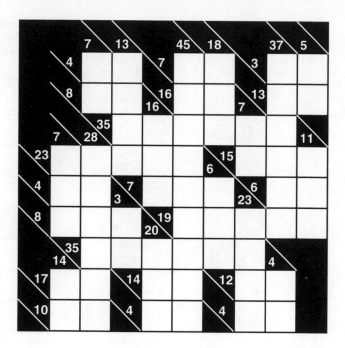

Puzzle 70: Easy

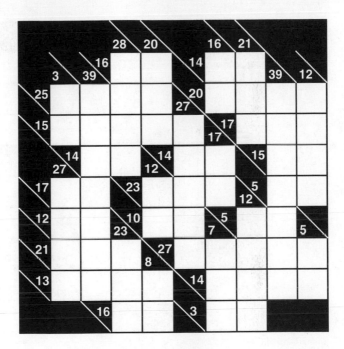

Puzzle 71: Easy

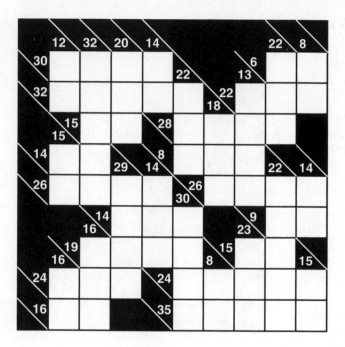

Puzzle 72: Easy

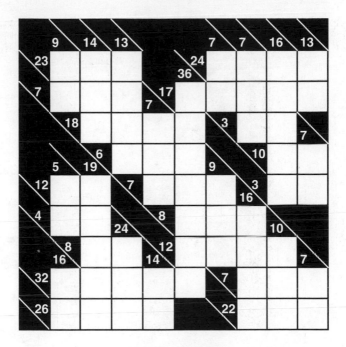

Puzzle 73: Easy

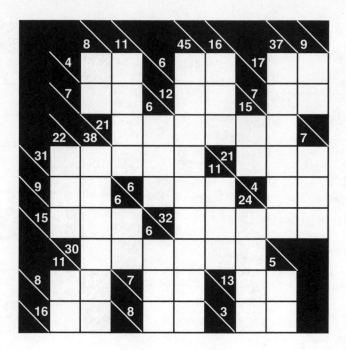

Puzzle 74: Easy

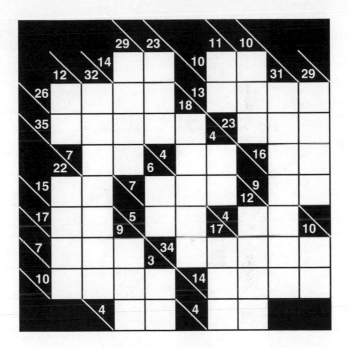

Puzzle 75: Easy

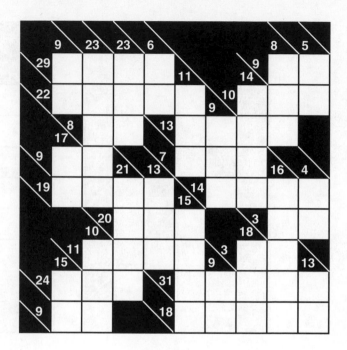

Puzzle 76: Easy

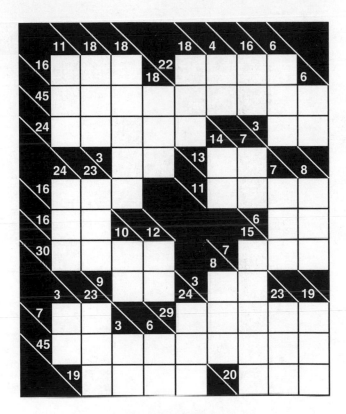

Puzzle 77: Easy

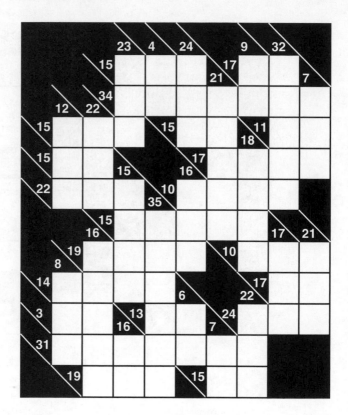

Puzzle 78: Easy

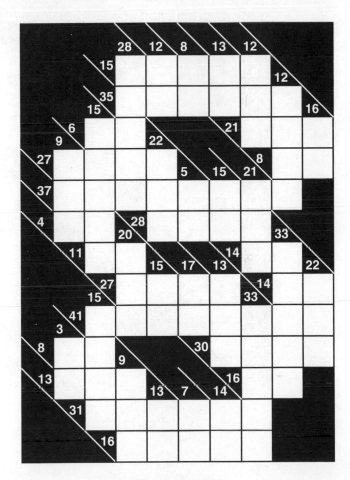

Puzzle 79: Easy

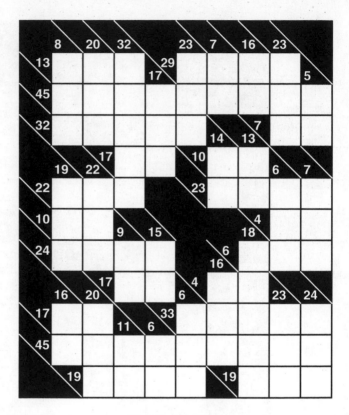

Puzzle 80: Easy

Puzzle 81: Easy

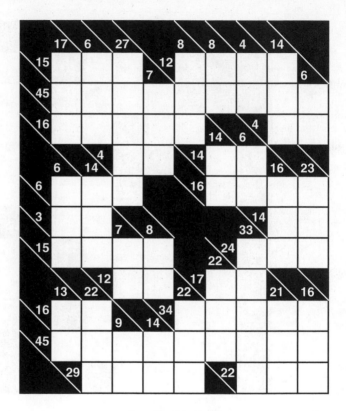

Puzzle 82: Easy

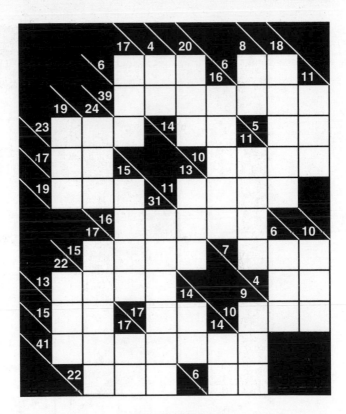

Puzzle 83: Easy

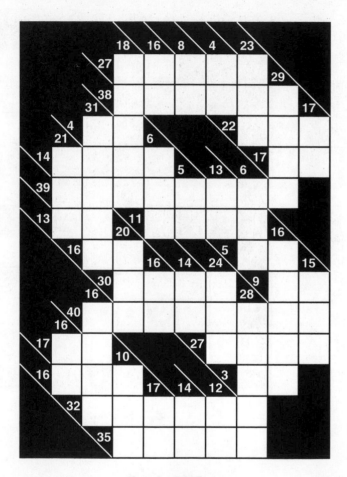

Puzzle 84: Easy

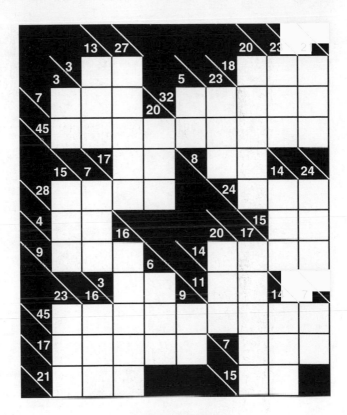

Puzzle 85: Easy

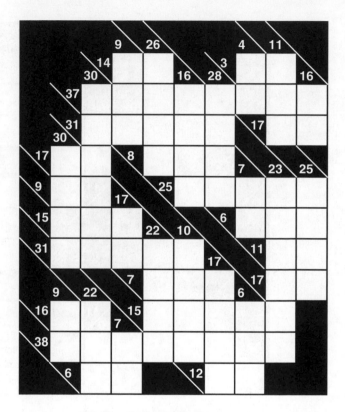

Puzzle 86: Easy

Puzzle 87: Easy

Puzzle 88: Easy

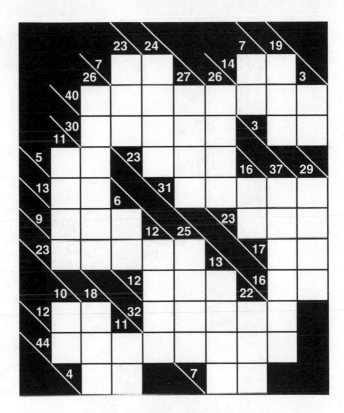

Puzzle 89: Easy

Puzzle 90: Easy

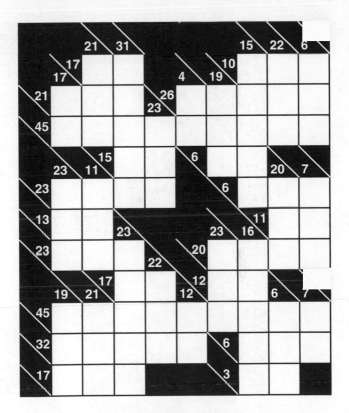

Puzzle 91: Easy

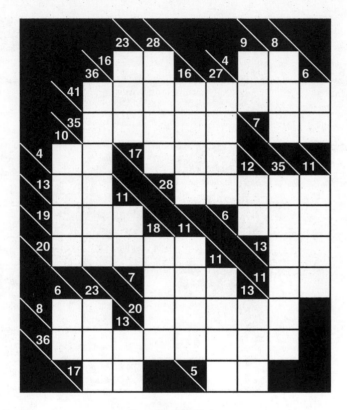

Puzzle 92: Easy

Puzzle 93: Easy

Puzzle 94: Easy

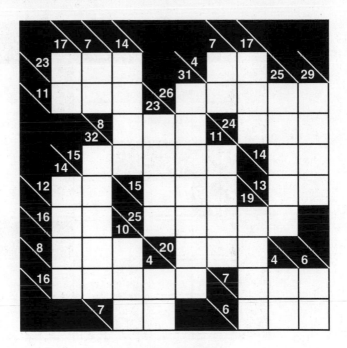

Puzzle 95: Easy

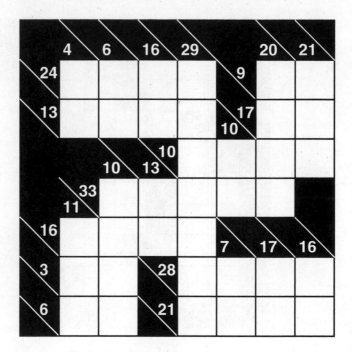

Puzzle 96: Easy

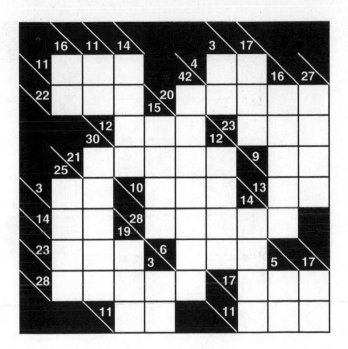

Puzzle 97: Easy

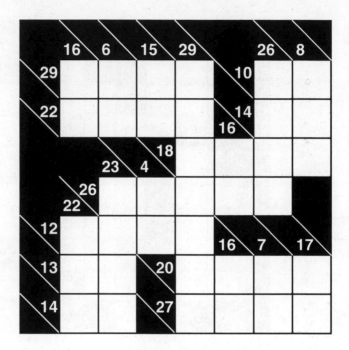

Puzzle 98: Easy

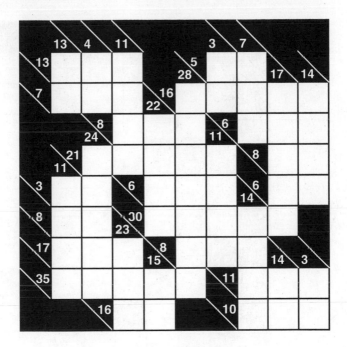

Puzzle 99: Easy

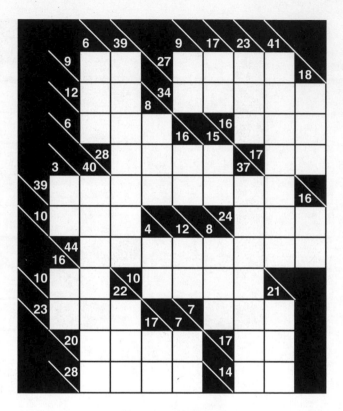

Puzzle 100: Easy

Puzzle 101: Easy

Puzzle 102: Easy

Puzzle 103: Easy

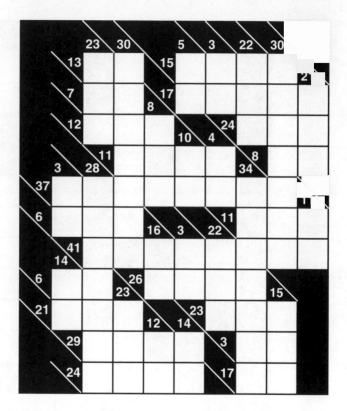

Puzzle 104: Easy

Puzzle 105: Easy

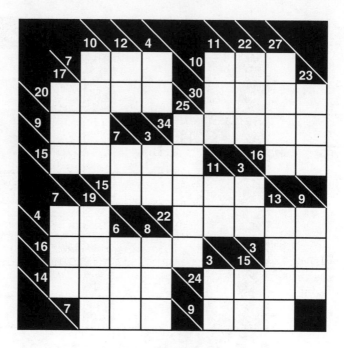

Puzzle 106: Easy

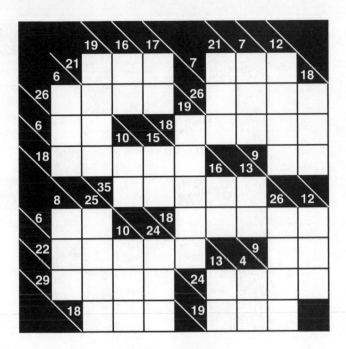

Puzzle 107: Easy

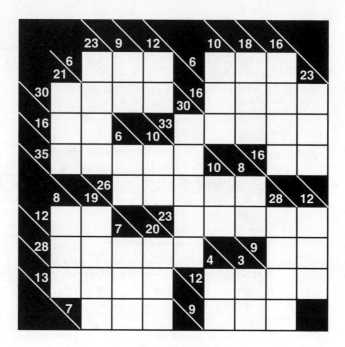

Puzzle 108: Easy

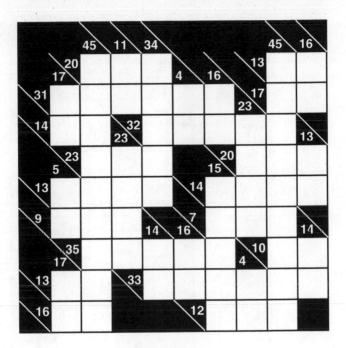

Puzzle 109: Easy

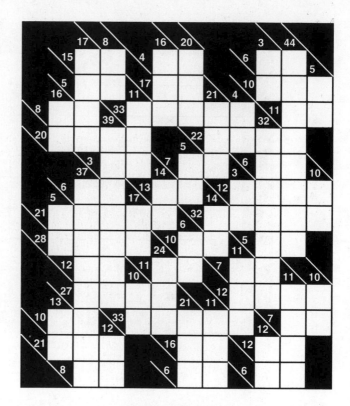

Puzzle 110: Easy

Getting Tricky

Puzzle 111: Medium

Puzzle 112: Medium

Puzzle 113: Medium

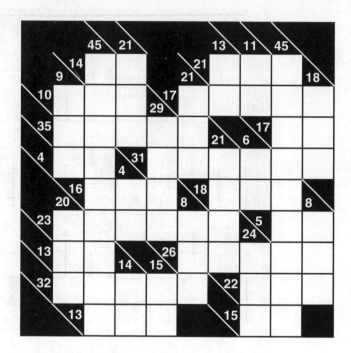

Puzzle 114: Medium

Puzzle 115: Medium

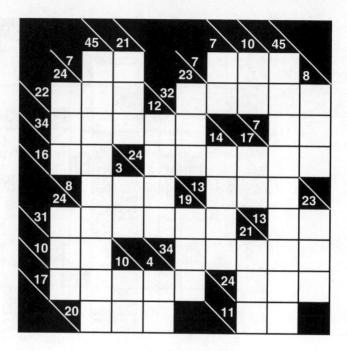

Puzzle 116: Medium

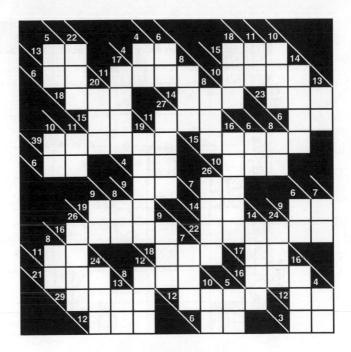

Puzzle 117: Medium

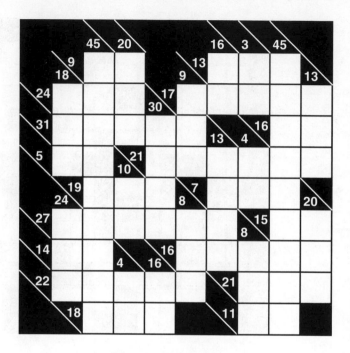

Puzzle 118: Medium

Puzzle 119: Medium

Puzzle 120: Medium

Puzzle 121: Medium

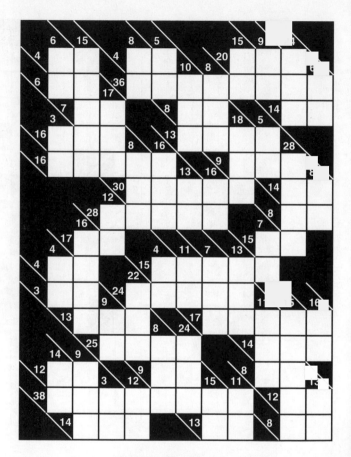

Puzzle 122: Medium

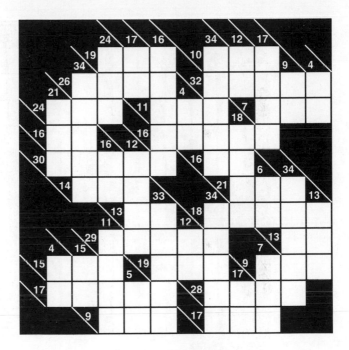

Puzzle 123: Medium

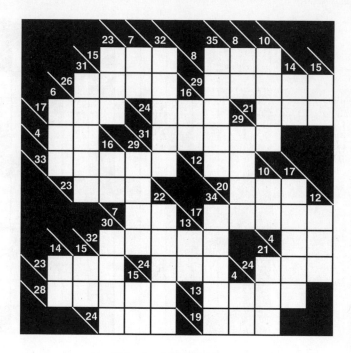

Puzzle 124: Medium

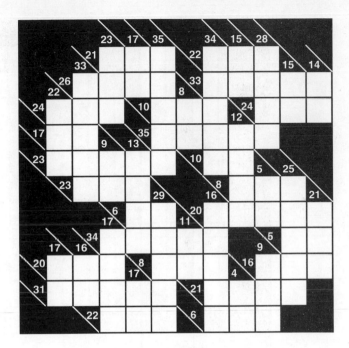

Puzzle 125: Medium

Puzzle 126: Medium

Puzzle 127: Medium

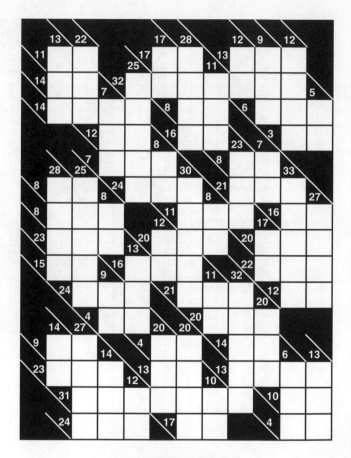

Puzzle 128: Medium

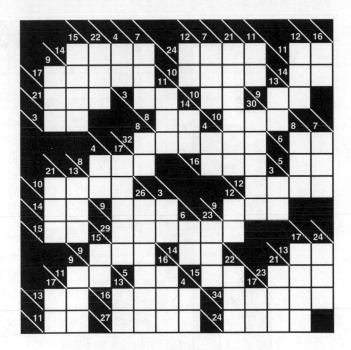

Puzzle 129: Medium

Puzzle 130: Medium

Puzzle 131: Medium

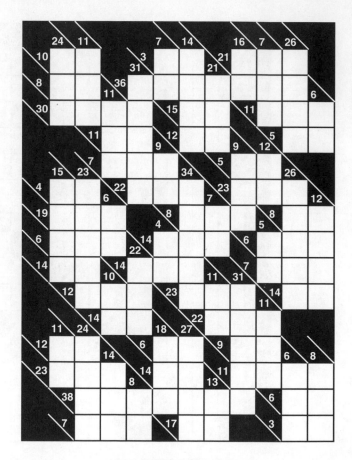

Puzzle 132: Medium

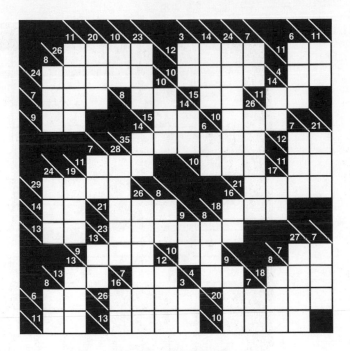

Puzzle 133: Medium

Puzzle 134: Medium

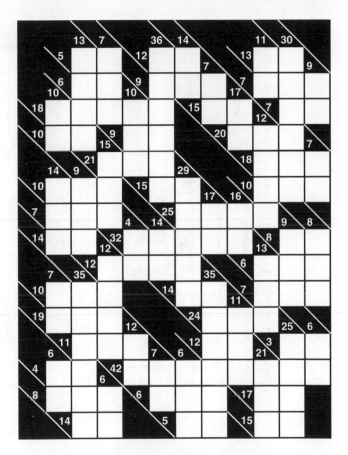

Puzzle 135: Medium

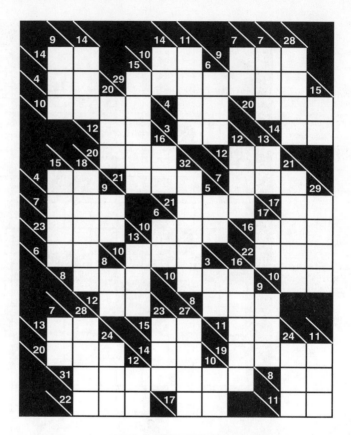

Puzzle 136: Medium

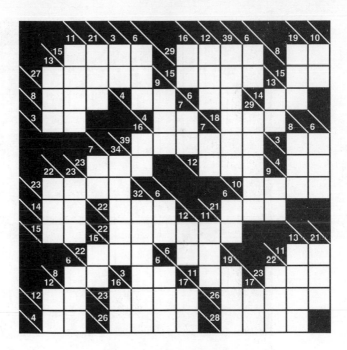

Puzzle 137: Medium

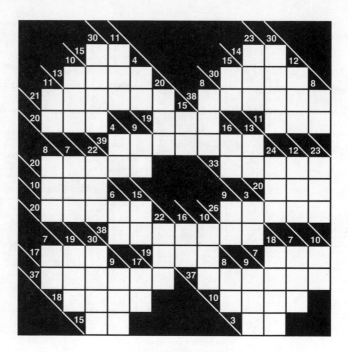

Puzzle 138: Medium

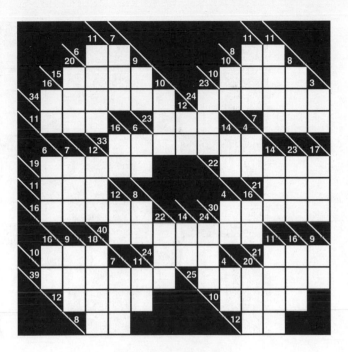

Puzzle 139: Medium

Puzzle 140: Medium

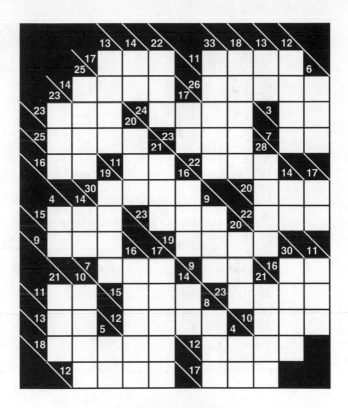

Puzzle 141: Medium

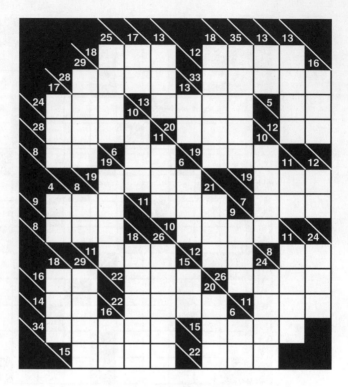

Puzzle 142: Medium

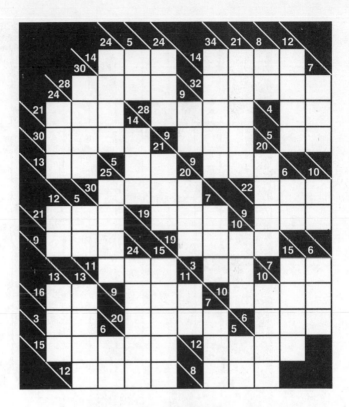

Puzzle 143: Medium

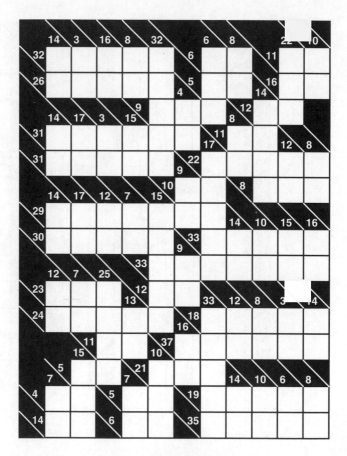

Puzzle 144: Medium

Puzzle 145: Medium

Puzzle 146: Medium

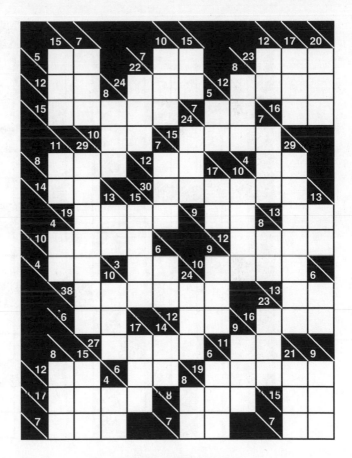

Puzzle 147: Medium

Puzzle 148: Medium

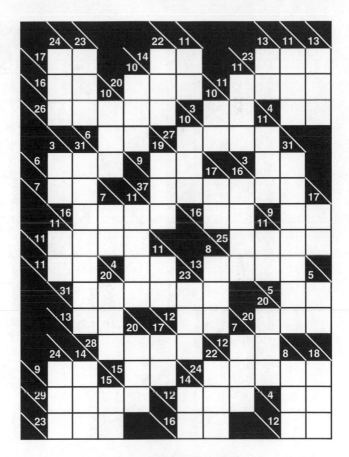

Puzzle 149: Medium

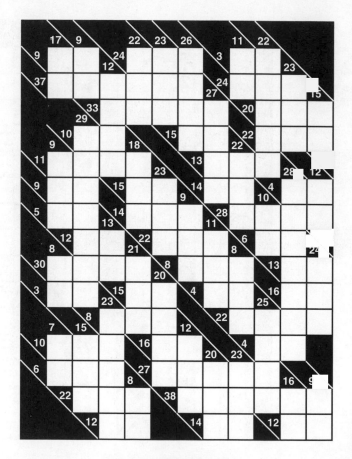

Puzzle 150: Medium

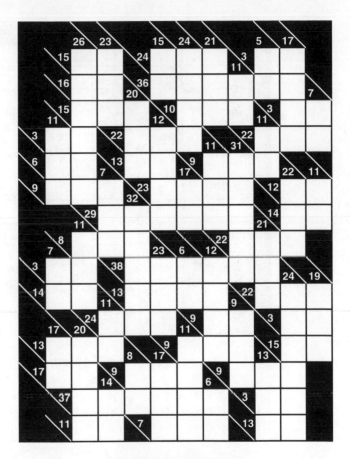

Puzzle 151: Medium

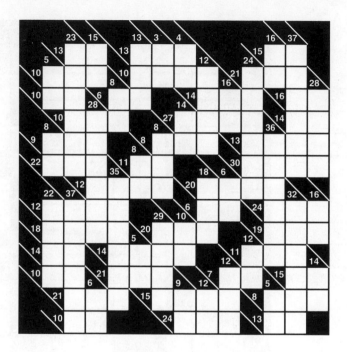

Puzzle 152: Medium

Puzzle 153: Medium

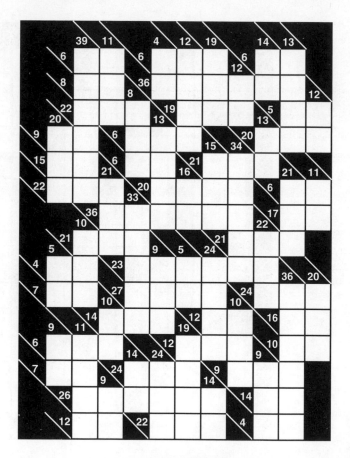

Puzzle 154: Medium

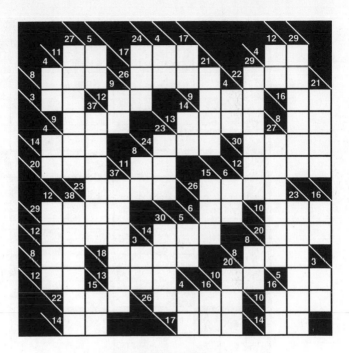

Puzzle 155: Medium

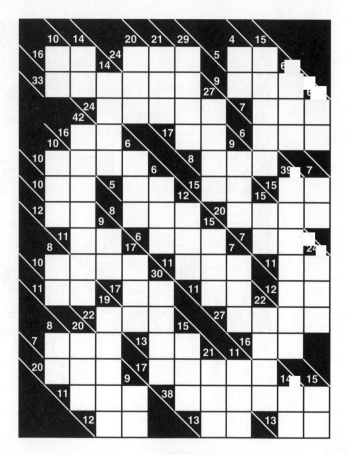

Puzzle 156: Medium

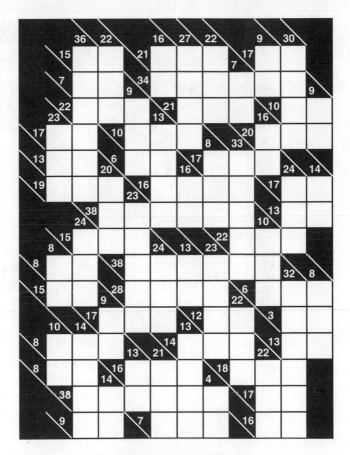

Puzzle 157: Medium

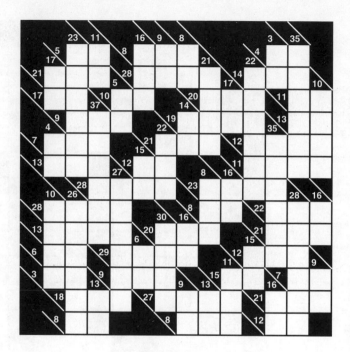

Puzzle 158: Medium

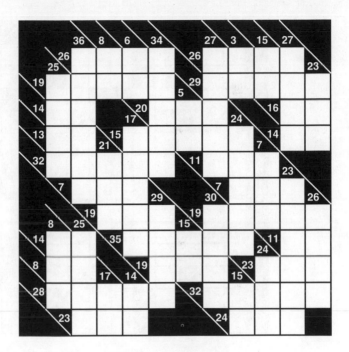

Puzzle 159: Medium

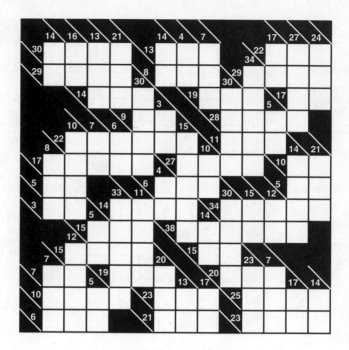

Puzzle 160: Medium

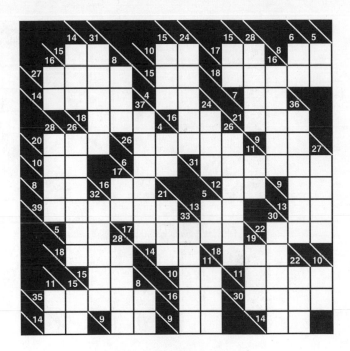

Puzzle 161: Medium

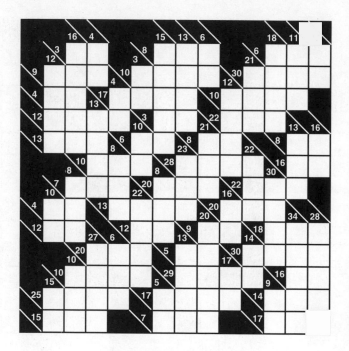

Puzzle 162: Medium

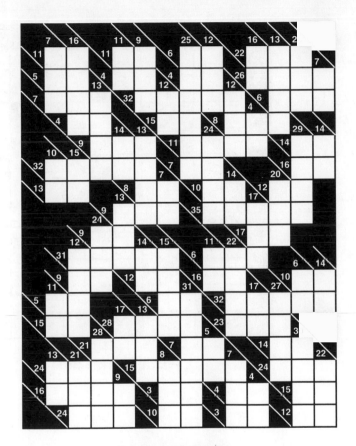

Puzzle 163: Medium

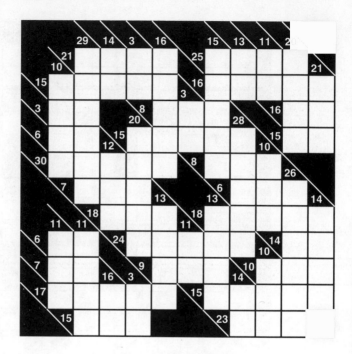

Puzzle 164: Medium

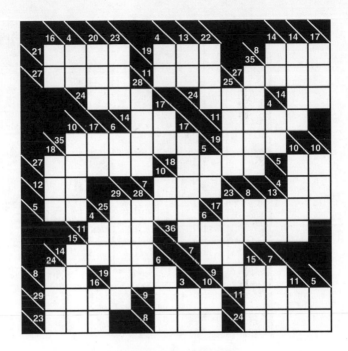

Puzzle 165: Medium

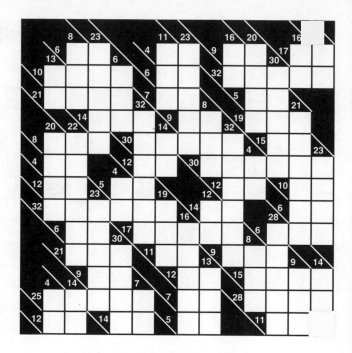

Puzzle 166: Medium

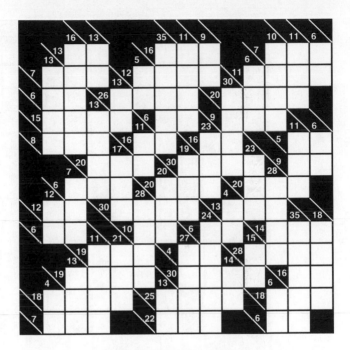

Puzzle 167: Medium

Puzzle 168: Medium

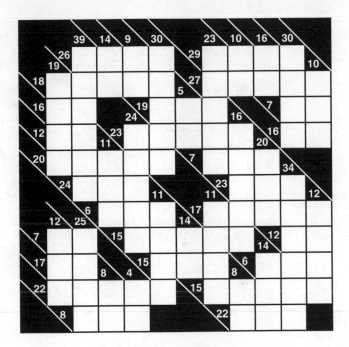

Puzzle 169: Medium

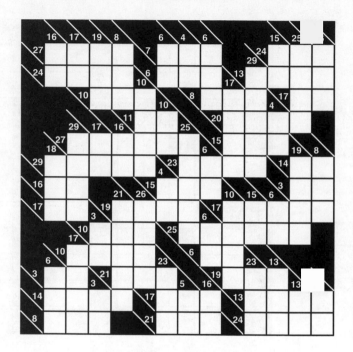

Puzzle 170: Medium

Tough Nuts to Crack

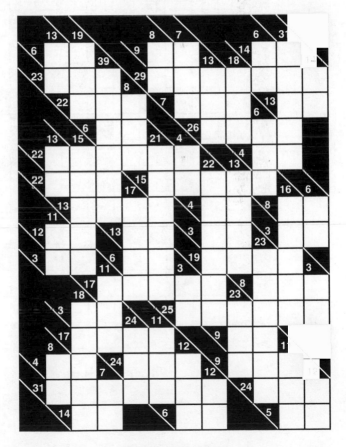

Puzzle 171: Hard

Puzzle 172: Hard

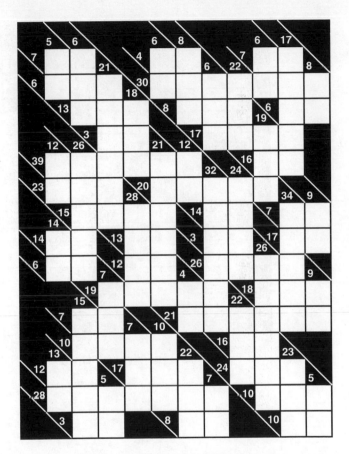

Puzzle 173: Hard

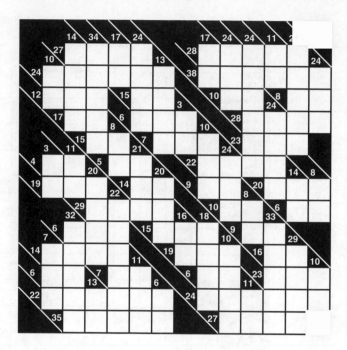

Puzzle 174: Hard

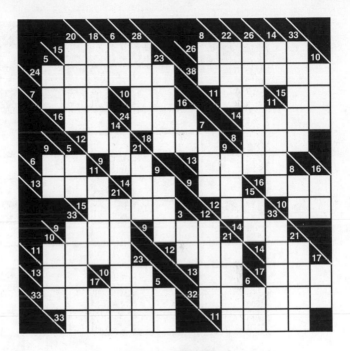

Puzzle 175: Hard

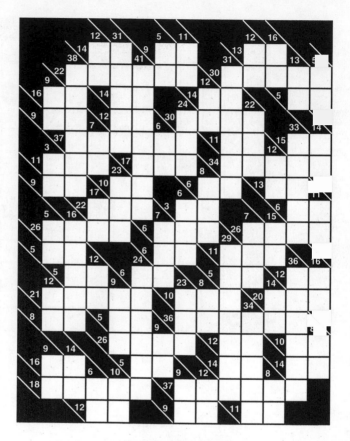

Puzzle 176: Hard

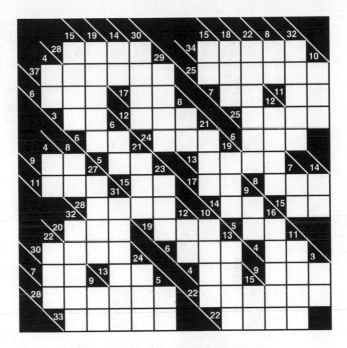

Puzzle 177: Hard

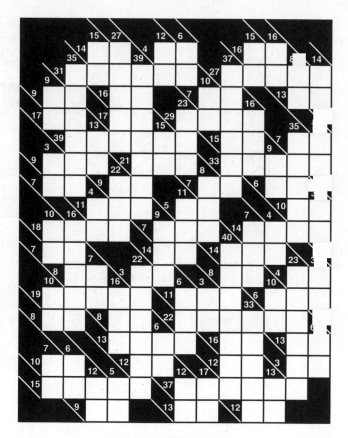

Puzzle 178: Hard

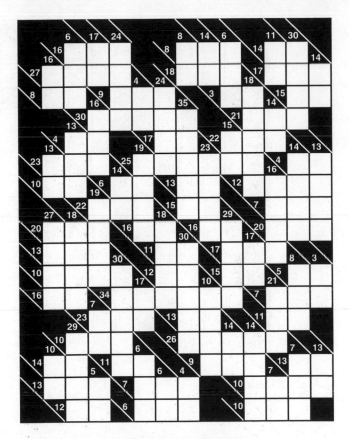

Puzzle 179: Hard

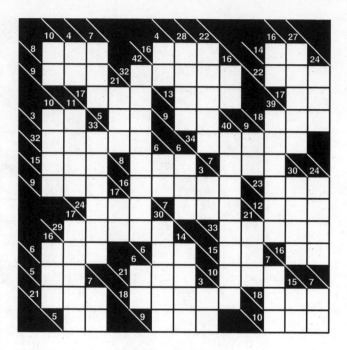

Puzzle 180: Hard

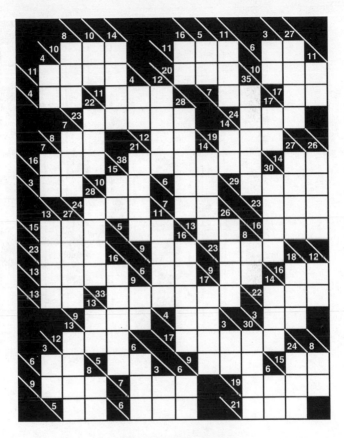

Puzzle 181: Hard

Puzzle 182: Hard

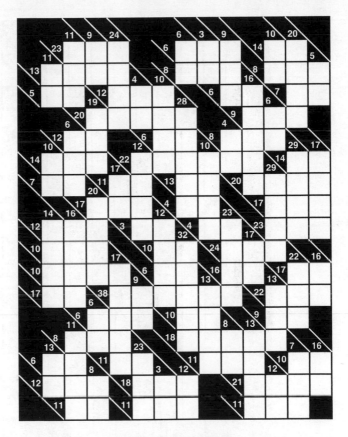

Puzzle 183: Hard

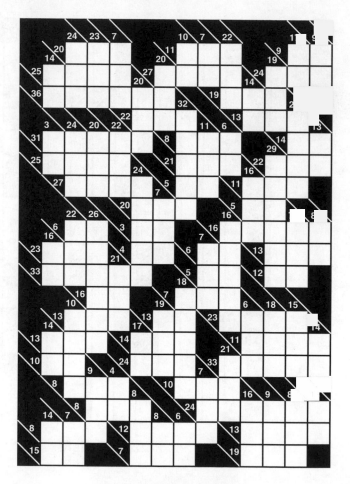

Puzzle 184: Hard

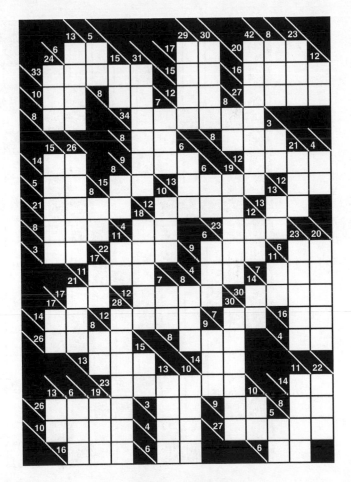

Puzzle 185: Hard

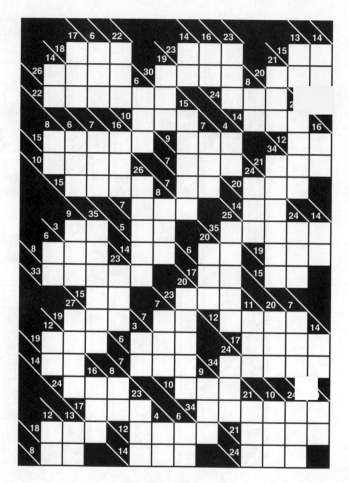

Puzzle 186: Hard

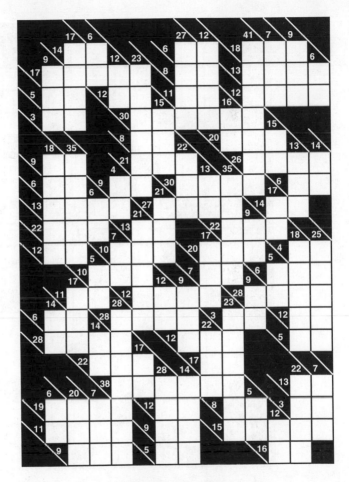

Puzzle 187: Hard

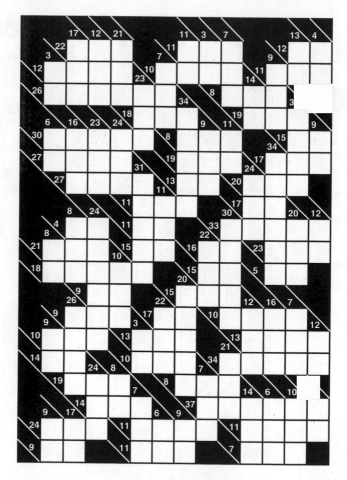

Puzzle 188: Hard

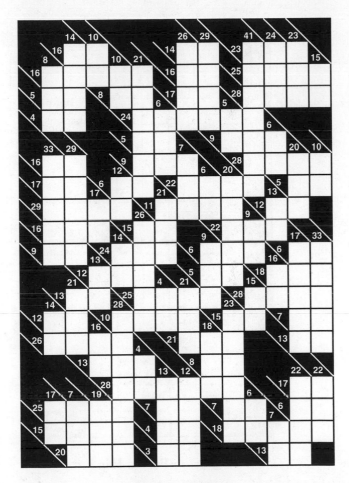

Puzzle 189: Hard

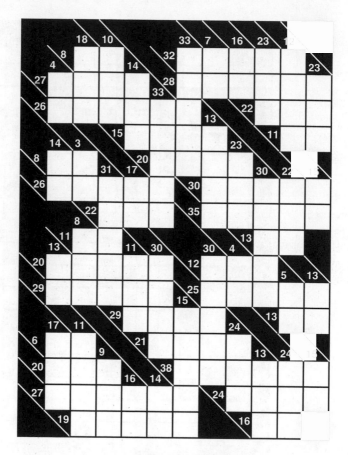

Puzzle 190: Hard

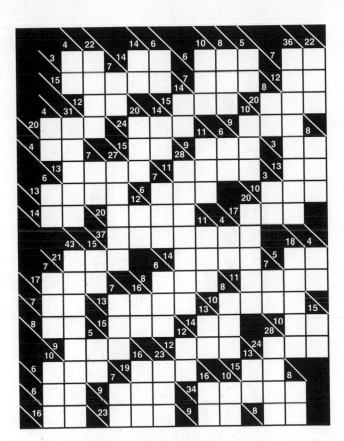

Puzzle 191: Hard

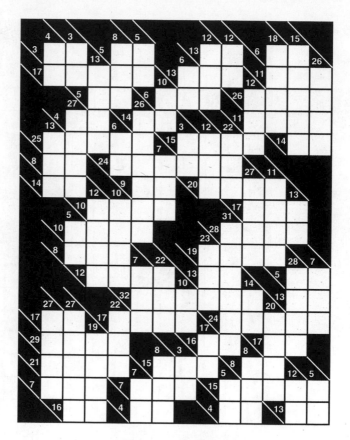

Puzzle 192: Hard

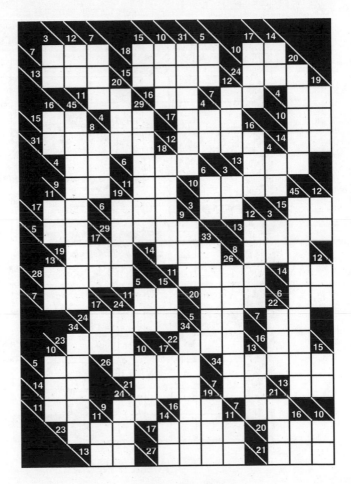

Puzzle 193: Hard

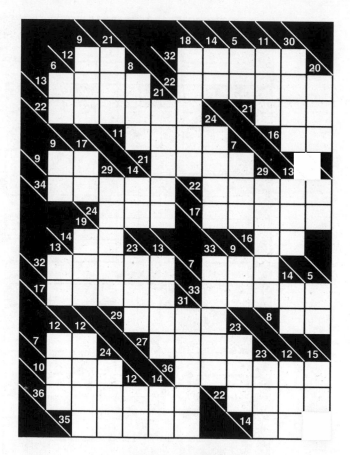

Puzzle 194: Hard

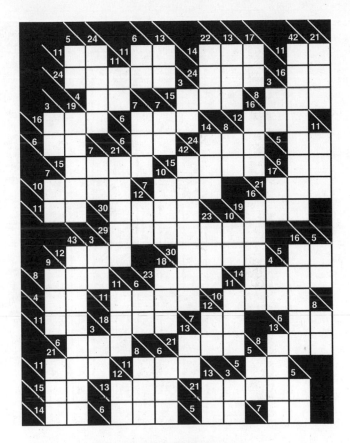

Puzzle 195: Hard

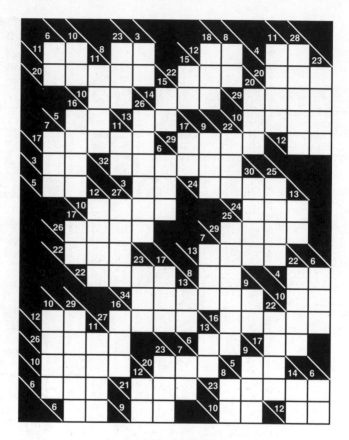

Puzzle 196: Hard

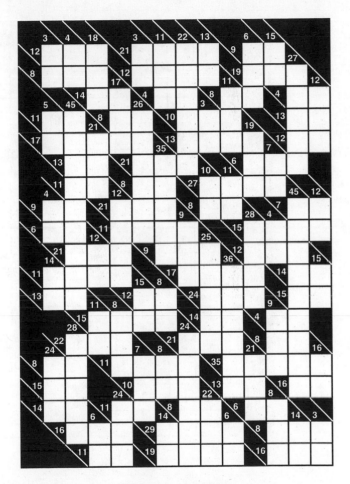

Puzzle 197: Hard

Puzzle 198: Hard

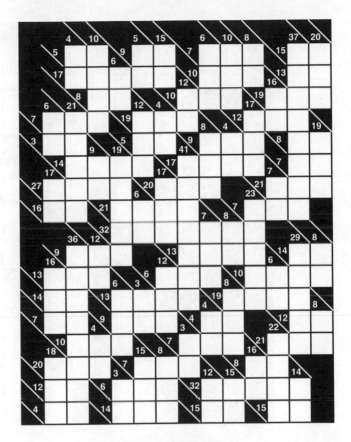

Puzzle 199: Hard

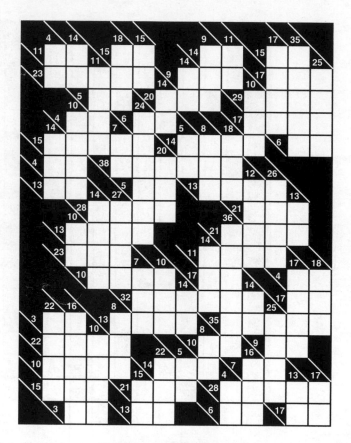

Puzzle 200: Hard

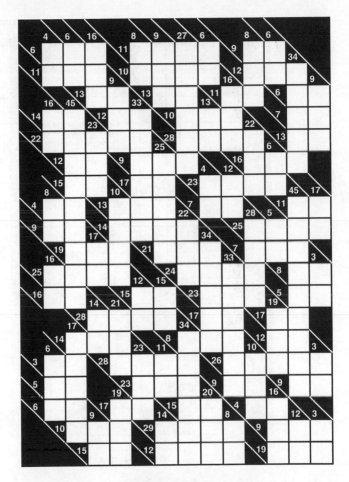

Puzzle 201: Hard

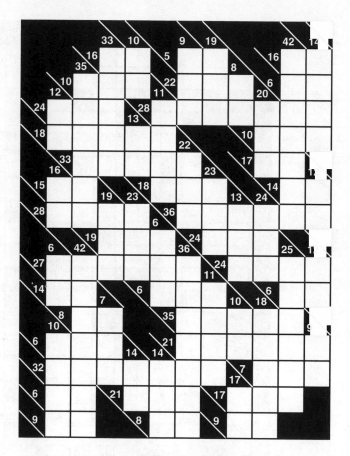

Puzzle 202: Hard

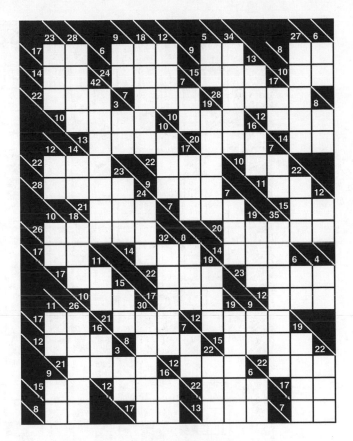

Puzzle 203: Hard

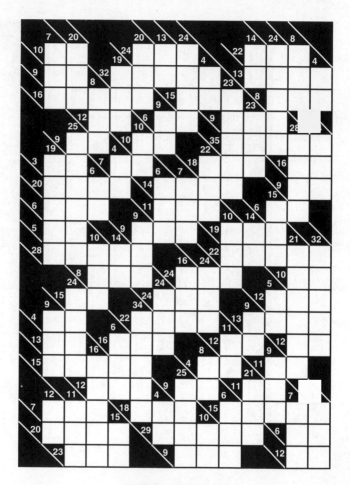

Puzzle 204: Hard

Puzzle 205: Hard

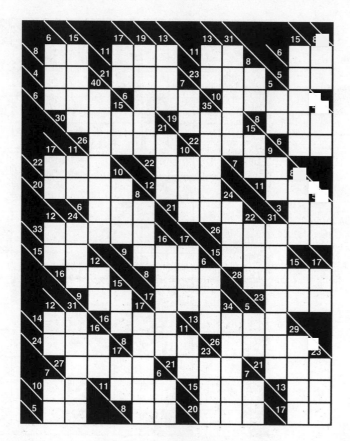

Puzzle 206: Hard

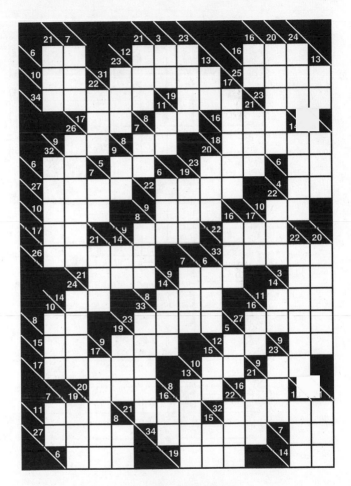

Puzzle 207: Hard

Puzzle 208: Hard

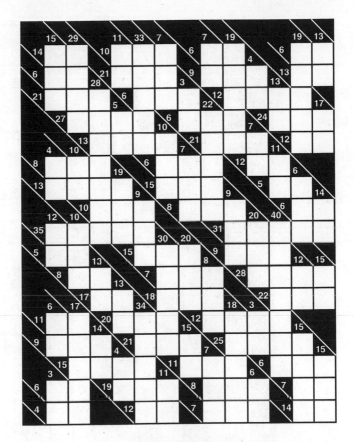

Puzzle 209: Hard

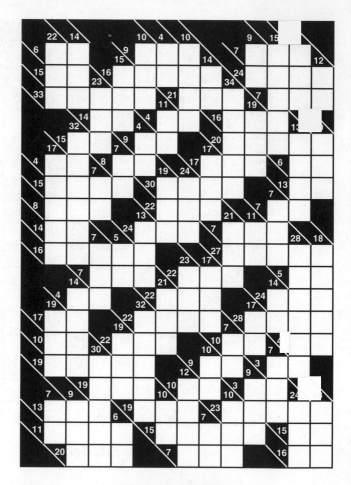

Puzzle 210: Hard

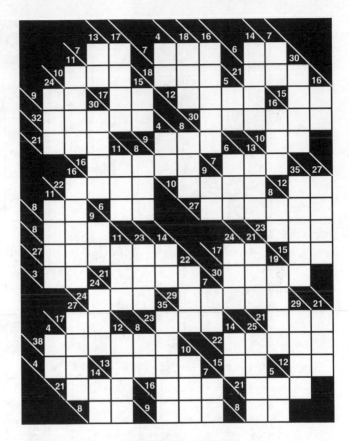

Puzzle 211: Hard

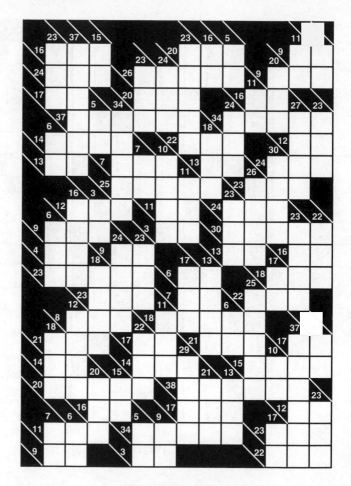

Puzzle 212: Hard

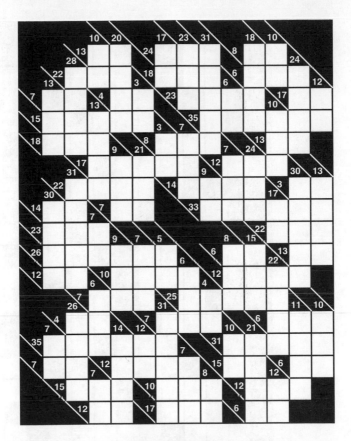

Puzzle 213: Hard

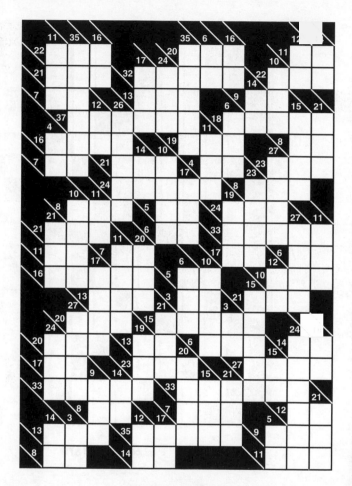

Puzzle 214: Hard

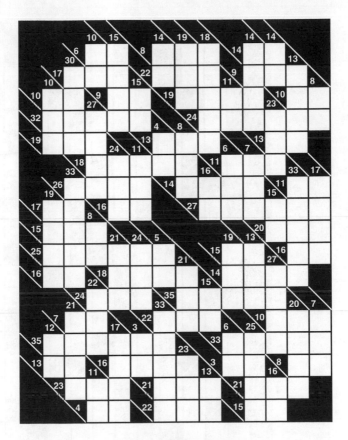

Puzzle 215: Hard

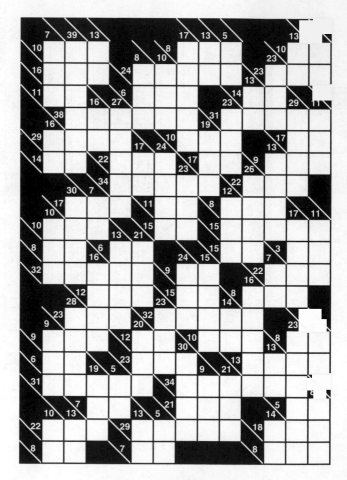

Puzzle 216: Hard

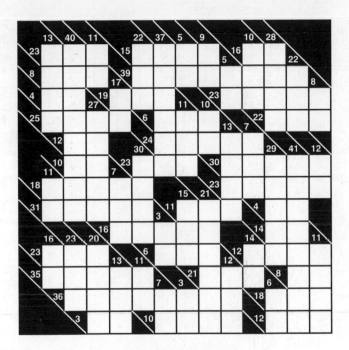

Puzzle 217: Hard

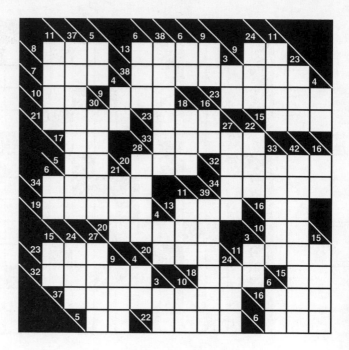

Puzzle 218: Hard

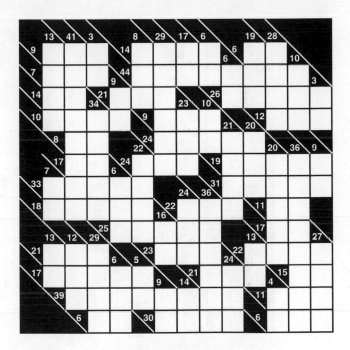

Puzzle 219: Hard

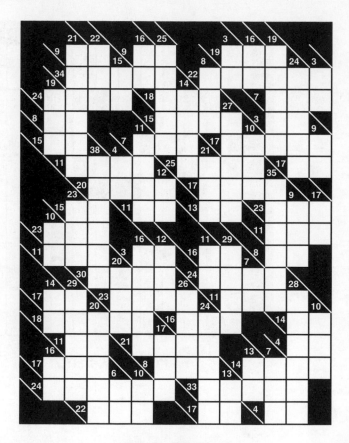

Puzzle 220: Hard

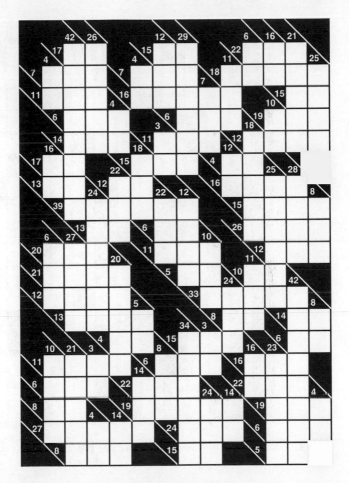

Puzzle 221: Hard

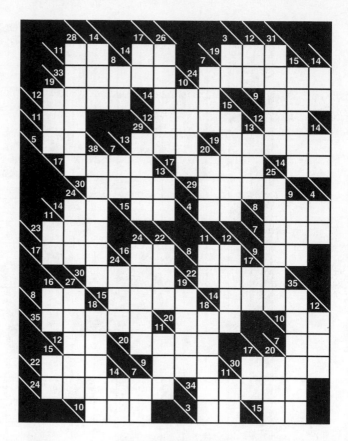

Puzzle 222: Hard

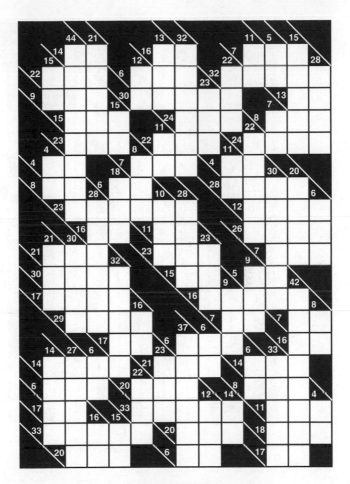

Puzzle 223: Hard

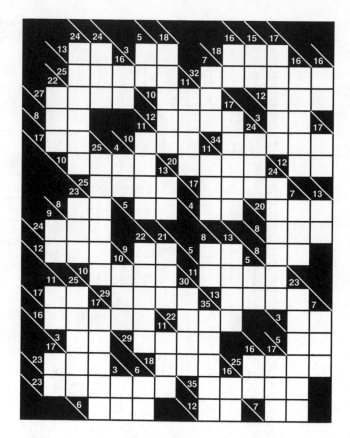

Puzzle 224: Hard

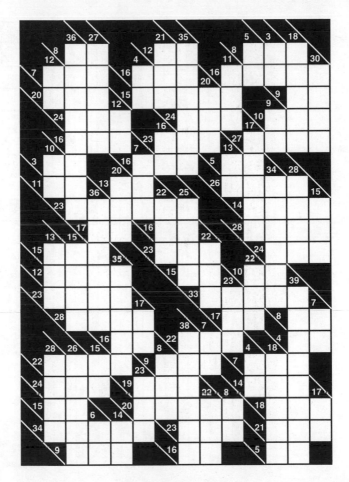

Puzzle 225: Hard

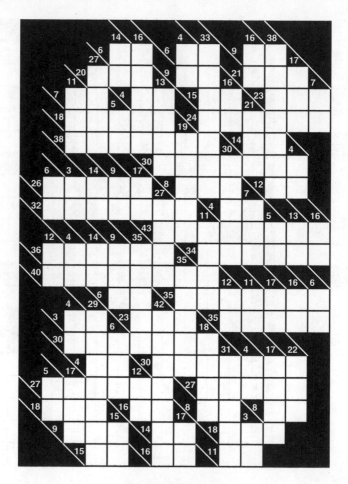

Puzzle 226: Hard

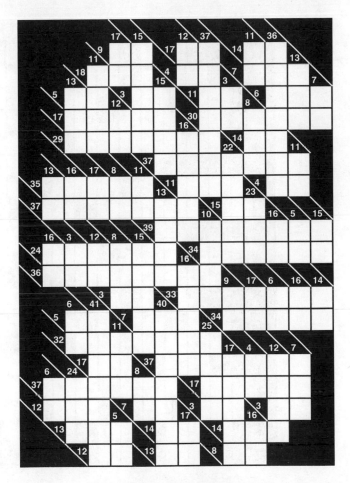

Puzzle 227: Hard

Puzzle 228: Hard

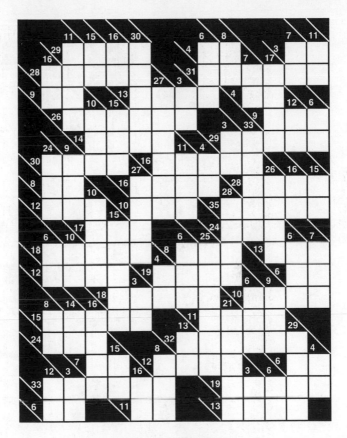

Puzzle 229: Hard

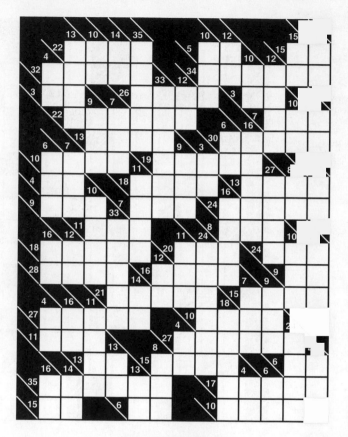

Puzzle 230: Hard

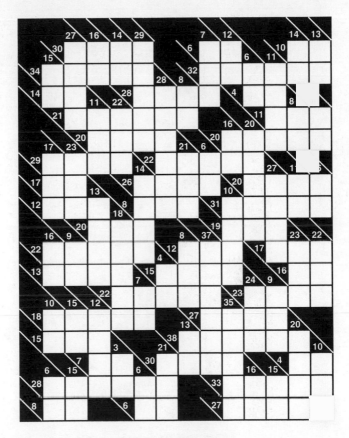

Puzzle 231: Hard

Diabolically Difficult

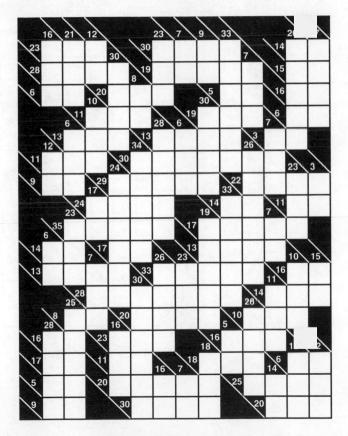

Puzzle 232: Diabolical

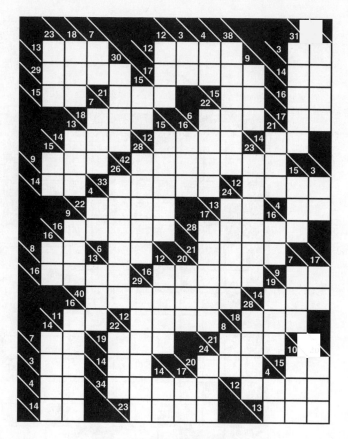

Puzzle 233: Diabolical

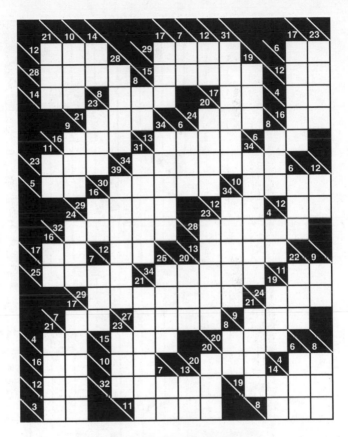

Puzzle 234: Diabolical

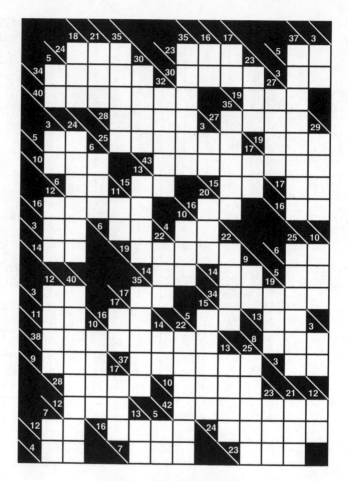

Puzzle 235: Diabolical

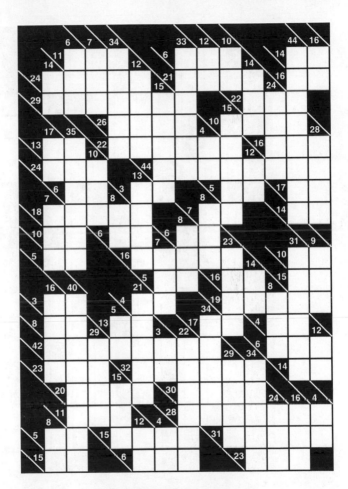

Puzzle 236: Diabolical

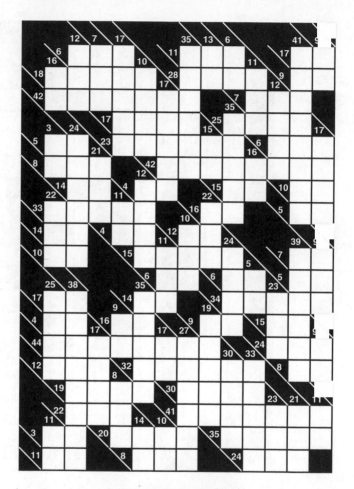

Puzzle 237: Diabolical

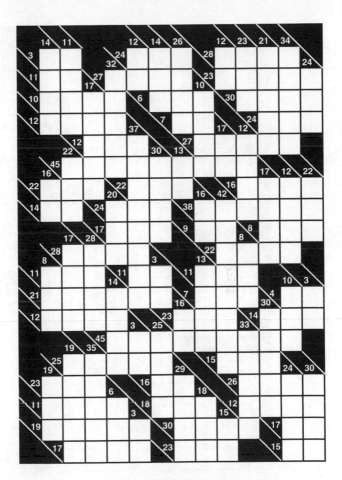

Puzzle 238: Diabolical

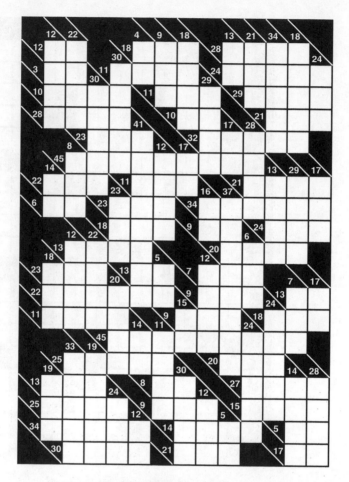

Puzzle 239: Diabolical

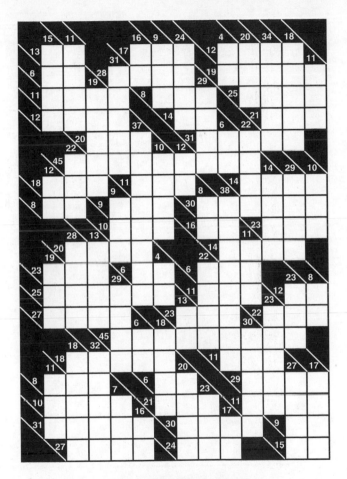

Puzzle 240: Diabolical

Part III

The Answer to Your Problems

The 5th Wave
By Rich Tennant

"What exactly does this have to do with Kakuro?"

In this part . . .

Having 240 puzzles to solve is all very well –
but only if we give you the answers too.
Here you'll find the solutions to all of the puzzles
in Part II. But remember, no cheating!

Easy Does It

Puzzle 1

5	9			3	1	
9	7	8		2	4	1
		9	8		2	4
	8	7	1	6	3	
1	6		2	8		
6	9	5		5	9	3
	7	9			7	8

Puzzle 2

9	8				1	3
1	2	6	7	3	5	9
	6	7	1		1	6
9	4				9	8
3	5		9	7	8	
7	3	1	5	9	6	8
	1	5			4	9

Puzzle 3

9	5			3	1	
7	9	8		2	3	1
		9	8		9	4
	3	6	9	5	7	
3	1		6	8		
2	4	3		1	2	3
	2	1			4	1

Puzzle 4

3	4				5	7
5	9	6		9	8	4
		7	9		9	8
	9	8	4	2	1	
3	2		7	9		
9	4	7		1	6	3
	1	9			4	2

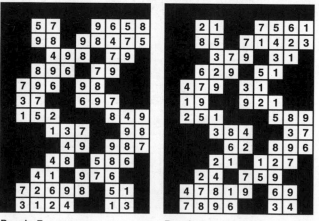

Puzzle 5

Puzzle 6

Puzzle 7

Puzzle 8

Puzzle 9

Puzzle 10

Puzzle 11

Puzzle 12

Puzzle 13

Puzzle 14

Puzzle 15

Puzzle 16

Puzzle 17

Puzzle 18

Puzzle 19

Puzzle 20

Puzzle 21

Puzzle 22

Puzzle 23

Puzzle 24

Puzzle 25

Puzzle 26

Puzzle 27

Puzzle 28

Puzzle 29

Puzzle 30

Puzzle 31

Puzzle 32

		7	8		1	4		
	9	8	6		5	9	8	6
7	4	9		2	3		1	7
9	8		3	5		6	2	
	7	3	2	1		3	4	2
4	5	2	1		4	2	3	1
9	6	5		7	8	5	9	
	3	1		8	9		6	4
3	1		7	5		9	5	8
1	2	3	5		6	8	7	
		5	9		1	7		

Puzzle 33

	6	7		1	3	2		
6	7	9		2	9	4	8	1
9	3		4	3			4	3
	5	6	9			7	[illegible]	[illegible]
6	8	9			2	5	[illegible]	[illegible]
3	4			9	5	8	6	7
4	1		2	4	1		2	6
5	9	2	1	7			5	8
		4	5			5	8	9
	5	1			3	1	7	
3	6			9	1		4	1
9	8	7	4	6		4	1	3
		8	6	7		5	9	

Puzzle 34

		2	5		9	8		
	9	1	7		5	1	9	3
9	7	4		9	6		2	4
5	3		6	8		2	5	
	6	8	9	5		1	3	4
1	8	5	7		8	4	6	9
3	1	9		8	9	5	7	
	5	7		6	5		1	8
1	2		5	9		4	8	7
6	4	8	9		2	1	4	
		6	7		5	3		

Puzzle 35

	3	6		9	7	5		
4	7	9		5	8	1	7	3
2	8		9	8			3	1
	2	6	8			7	[illegible]	[illegible]
4	5	7			1	4	[illegible]	[illegible]
8	6			1	5	9	7	2
9	4		7	2	6		2	3
7	1	2	9	6			3	1
		1	4			9	5	4
	8	6			7	8	4	
2	4			7	5		6	2
7	9	4	5	8		1	8	6
		1	3	4		4	9	

Puzzle 36

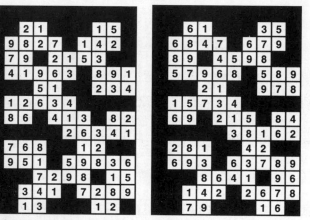

Puzzle 37

Puzzle 38

Puzzle 39

Puzzle 40

Puzzle 41

Puzzle 42

Puzzle 43

Puzzle 44

Puzzle 45

Puzzle 46

Puzzle 47

Puzzle 48

Puzzle 49

Puzzle 50

Puzzle 51

Puzzle 52

Puzzle 53

Puzzle 54

Puzzle 55

Puzzle 56

Puzzle 57

	9	2			9	8	
7	2	5	4	8	6	9	
9	7			9	7		
5	4	9		4	1	9	
	3	2			3	8	
1	5	8	6	3	2	4	
3	1		8	9			

Puzzle 58

1	2			9	6		
3	4	5	9	8	7	6	
	6	9	8		8	9	
3	7				5	8	
1	3		1	3	4		
5	1	7	3	2	9	8	
	5	9			3	1	

Puzzle 59

	7	6	8	9				
5	9	4	2	7	8		9	7
1	4			9	6	1	4	2
	1	6	2		2	6	9	
1	5	3	2		3	4	8	
5	9	6		7	9	6		
3	6	4	2	1			1	3
2	1		3	9	8	1	5	2
		9	6	7	5			

Puzzle 60

9	7		2	1		3	9	5
8	9		6	2		2	5	1
2	5	1	3		7	9		
		2	5	8	4	7	3	6
6	8		4	9	8		1	2
8	7	4	9	6	1	3		
		5	1		2	1	4	3
9	3	1		7	3		1	6
3	1	2		8	6		3	1

		1	6		7	9
5	1	2	9	4	3	7
9	8			2	5	
1	4	2		1	6	2
	9	3			2	1
2	6	1	7	8	9	5
4	7		5	9		

Puzzle 61

1	5			6	9	
3	4	1	6	9	5	8
	1	2	3		6	9
1	2				1	3
2	3		1	5	2	
3	6	8	2	9	4	7
	8	9			7	9

Puzzle 62

		7	9	8	1			
7	5	9	8	6	2		3	7
9	3			9	6	5	1	8
		8	9	7		8	9	6
6	9	5	7		1	9	7	
7	8	9		1	2	6		
8	4	7	9	5			2	4
9	7		7	3	5	2	1	6
			8	2	3	1		

Puzzle 63

3	1		9	8		3	1	2
2	4		7	9		8	3	4
1	2	3	6		9	5		
		1	8	9	4	2	3	5
5	3		4	8	6		1	2
9	1	6	5	7	3	8		
		1	2		5	6	1	9
2	4	5		9	1		2	6
1	2	4		7	2		7	8

Puzzle 64

1	4	2			9	3	4	8
7	8	5		1	5	2	3	4
	6	3	9	8		1	5	
		1	2	3			1	5
7	8		1	7	9		2	9
8	4			5	8	2		
	9	3		2	6	3	1	
1	6	2	3	4		4	6	9
3	5	1	4			1	2	8

Puzzle 65

	8	9		3	1		3	9
	9	5		6	2		1	6
		6	1	5	3	2	4	
5	9	8	4	7		6	9	8
3	2		3	4	1		7	9
1	5	2		9	6	1	2	4
	4	1	3	8	5	2		
8	7		4	1		3	1	
4	1		1	2		5	6	

Puzzle 66

		2	1		9	7		
4	8	9	2		2	1	8	5
1	5	4	3	2		2	5	1
	1	3		5	3		6	9
7	9		1	8	2		2	3
3	7		3	1		9	7	
1	6	7		6	5	4	3	1
2	3	4	1		2	8	9	4
		9	8		9	7		

Puzzle 67

2	9	4	3				9	8
3	8	2	1	9		9	8	6
	2	1		6	9	7	2	
2	4			8	4	2		
3	6	1	4		7	8	9	5
		3	9	7			8	3
	9	5	7	8		2	3	
1	4	2		1	9	3	5	2
9	7			9	8	4	7	5

Puzzle 68

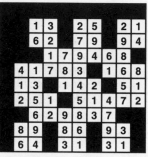

Puzzle 69

Puzzle 70

Puzzle 71

Puzzle 72

Puzzle 73

Puzzle 74

Puzzle 75

Puzzle 76

Puzzle 77

Puzzle 78

Puzzle 79

Puzzle 80

Puzzle 81

Puzzle 82

Puzzle 83

Puzzle 84

Puzzle 85

Puzzle 86

Puzzle 87

Puzzle 88

Puzzle 89

		6	1			6	8		
	4	8	6	3	7	1	9	2	
	1	9	8	7	5		2	1	
3	2		9	8	6				
5	8			9	8	7	2	5	
1	6	2			9	6	8		
2	5	4	3	9		8	9		
		1	5	6		9	7		
4	8		6	8	2	9	7		
6	9	8	2	3	4	7	5		
	1	3			1	6			

Puzzle 90

3	5	9			2	9			
2	1	7	3		1	8	4	2	
		8	4	9			6	1	
	6	1	7	5	9	8	3		
1	5	3	2		1	7	3		
4	9	5			6	5			
3	4					9	7		
	7	5			3	1	2		
	2	8	1		8	6	7	1	
7	3	9	4	8	1	5			
9	8			7	9	8			
5	6	8	1		4	1	9	7	
		9	4			2	8	9	

Puzzle 91

	9	8				3	6	1
8	7	6		1	8	5	9	3
9	5	1	8	3	6	4	7	2
	9	6		5	1			
6	1	7	9			2	3	1
9	4					9	2	
8	6	9		6	2	8	4	
	8	9		8	4			
2	8	1	7	4	9	6	3	5
9	7	2	6	8		3	1	2
8	6	3			1	2		

Puzzle 92

		9	7			3	1	
	7	8	9	2	3	6	5	1
	5	6	8	7	9		2	5
1	3		4	6	7			
4	9			1	8	9	7	3
2	8	9			3	2	1	
3	4	2	6	5		8	5	
		4	2	1		9	2	
2	6		7	1	5	4	3	
4	8	5	1	3	2	7	6	
	9	8			3	2		

Puzzle 93

Puzzle 94

Puzzle 95

Puzzle 96

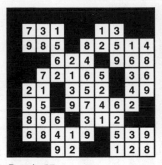

Puzzle 97

Puzzle 98

Puzzle 99

Puzzle 100

Puzzle 101

Puzzle 102

Puzzle 103

Puzzle 104

4	2	1	8			8	2	1
2	1	5	6		1	3	5	2
		2	4	1	3	5		
1	3		1	5	4			
2	1	3	5		2	9	7	
	4	1	2		7	8	5	9
1	7						8	7
4	8	9	2		1	2	4	
	2	4	1		6	4	9	3
			8	6	9		6	1
		4	3	1	8	9		
9	8	2	7		2	5	1	3
7	9	1			7	6	2	9

Puzzle 105

	2	4	1		1	6	3	
5	4	8	3		6	7	9	8
8	1			7	4	9	8	6
4	3	2	1	5			7	9
		5	2	3	4	1		
1	3			9	7	2	3	1
4	6	2	3	1			1	2
2	8	3	1		2	9	7	6
	2	1	4		1	6	2	

Puzzle 106

	4	9	8		4	2	1	
2	8	7	9		9	4	5	8
1	5			2	8	1	4	3
3	2	4	8	1			2	7
		6	7	5	9	8		
1	5			3	7	5	2	1
2	4	1	7	8			7	2
5	9	7	8		6	1	8	9
	7	2	9		7	3	9	

Puzzle 107

	1	2	3		1	2	3	
8	6	7	9		2	7	1	6
7	9			4	7	9	5	8
6	7	5	8	9			7	9
		1	2	8	9	6		
5	7			3	1	2	9	8
1	8	4	9	6			8	1
2	3	1	7		1	2	6	3
	1	2	4		3	1	5	

Puzzle 108

Puzzle 109

Puzzle 110

Getting Tricky

Puzzle 111

Puzzle 112

Puzzle 113

Puzzle 114

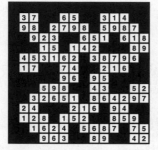

Puzzle 115

Puzzle 116

Puzzle 117

Puzzle 118

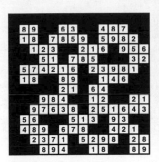

Puzzle 119

Puzzle 120

Puzzle 121

Puzzle 122

Puzzle 123

Puzzle 124

Puzzle 125

Puzzle 126

Puzzle 127

Puzzle 128

Puzzle 129

Puzzle 130

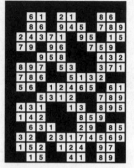

Puzzle 131

Puzzle 132

Puzzle 133

Puzzle 134

Puzzle 135

Puzzle 136

Puzzle 137

Puzzle 138

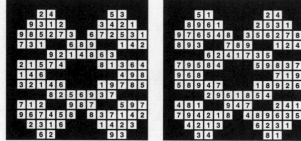

Puzzle 139

Puzzle 140

Puzzle 141

Puzzle 142

		4	1	9		7	4	1	2	
	8	9	4	7		8	9	7	6	2
9	7	5		8	6	9	5		3	1
8	9	6	7		3	4	2		1	4
7	6		1	4		6	1	2		
		9	6	8	7			9	5	8
9	4	8		9	8	2		6	1	2
3	1	5			5	4	7	3		
		3	7	1		1	2		6	1
9	7		1	3	5		1	4	3	2
1	2		8	5	6	1		2	1	3
3	1	5	2	4		2	4	1	5	
	3	1	6	2		4	1	3		

Puzzle 143

8	2	7	6	9		1	5		8	3
6	1	9	2	8		2	3		9	7
				5	1	3		7	5	
5	9	2	8	4	3		7	4		
9	8	1	7	6		6	1	2	8	5
					8	2		1	4	3
6	8	5	2	4	1	3				
8	9	7	5	1		5	9	4	8	7
				3	2	1	5	6	7	9
8	6	9		5	7					
4	1	8	9	2		4	5	2	1	6
		7	4		9	5	7	6	2	8
	4	1		6	7	8				
1	3		2	3		7	6	3	1	2
6	8		5	1		9	8	7	5	6

Puzzle 144

7	9			3	2			9	7	8
1	5		9	2	4		7	6	9	5
2	4	6	3	1		8	9		8	9
		1	7		7	9	5	6		
8	6	3		2	9			1	3	
7	2			1	5	4	7	3	2	
	4	7	1	3		8	2		1	3
8	7	9	2				9	8	5	7
2	9		8	9		9	8	7	6	
	8	9	4	6	3	7			7	3
	5	3			4	8		2	4	9
		6	3	1	2		9	3		
8	9		9	6		4	7	5	9	8
9	7	5	8		9	8	5		5	2
6	8	9			6	5			7	1

Puzzle 145

2	3	5	1	4		5	9		4	7
6	1	4	2	3		1	4		1	4
				1	3	2		5	2	
3	7	9	1	2	8		2	4		
1	3	6	2	5		8	1	2	6	3
					9	7		1	9	2
4	9	3	5	7	8	6				
2	6	1	3	4		9	8	6	7	5
				6	9	3	2	8	4	1
1	3	2		1	5					
5	1	3	9	2		4	1	8	3	2
		1	5		4	3	6	5	2	1
	1	5		1	2	7				
6	2		9	5		2	6	9	1	8
2	4		7	3		6	8	7	3	9

Puzzle 146

Puzzle 147

Puzzle 148

Puzzle 149

Puzzle 150

Puzzle 151

Puzzle 152

Puzzle 153

Puzzle 154

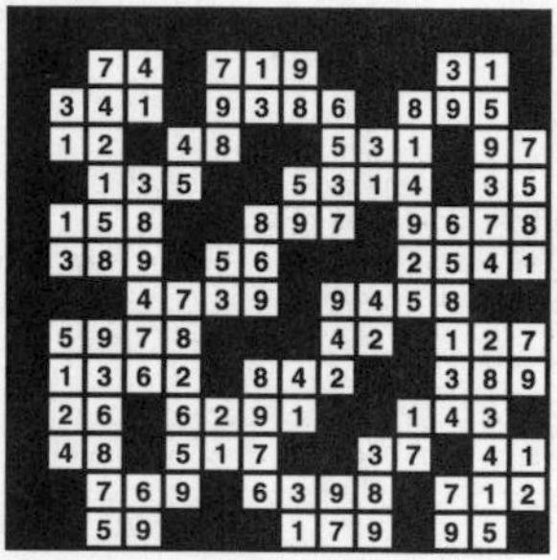

Puzzle 155

Puzzle 156

Puzzle 157

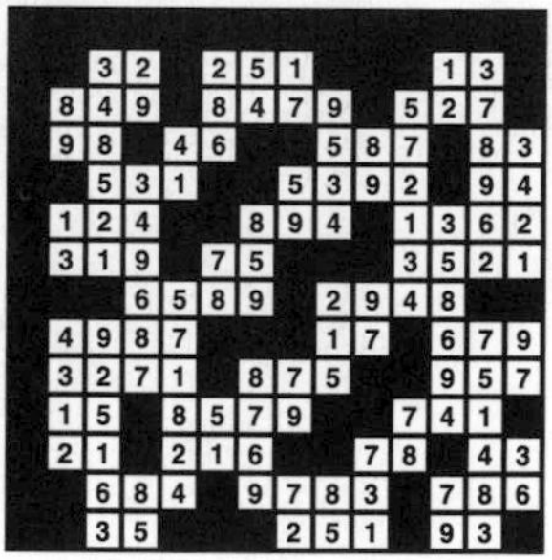

Puzzle 158

Puzzle 159

Puzzle 160

Puzzle 161

Puzzle 162

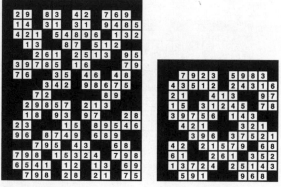

Puzzle 163

Puzzle 164

Puzzle 165

Puzzle 166

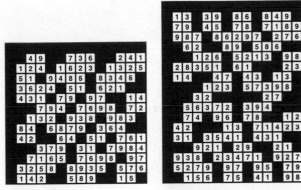

Puzzle 167

Puzzle 168

Puzzle 169

Puzzle 170

Tough Nuts to Crack

Puzzle 171

Puzzle 172

Puzzle 173

Puzzle 174

Puzzle 175

Puzzle 176

Puzzle 177

Puzzle 178

Puzzle 179

Puzzle 180

Puzzle 181

Puzzle 182

Puzzle 183

Puzzle 184

Puzzle 185

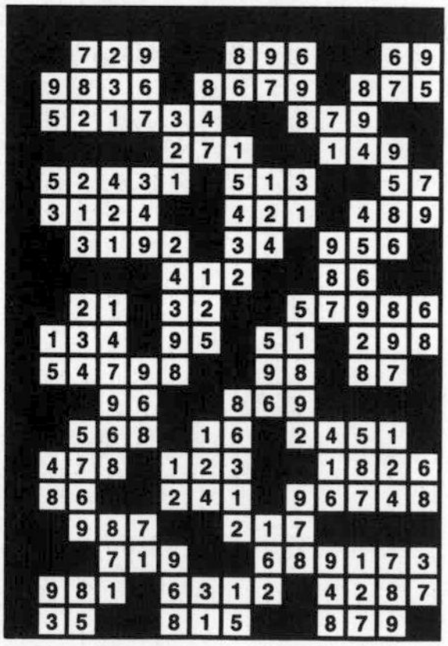

Puzzle 186

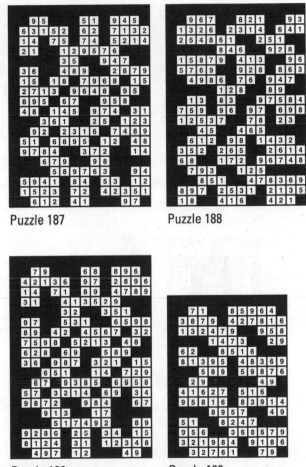

Puzzle 187

Puzzle 188

Puzzle 189

Puzzle 190

Puzzle 191

Puzzle 192

Puzzle 193

Puzzle 194

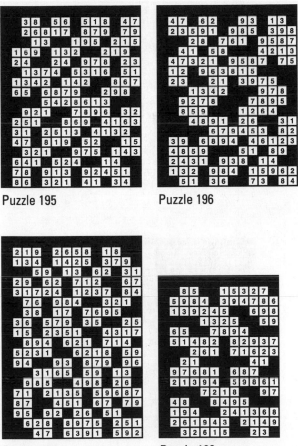

Puzzle 195

Puzzle 196

Puzzle 197

Puzzle 198

Puzzle 199

Puzzle 200

Puzzle 201

Puzzle 202

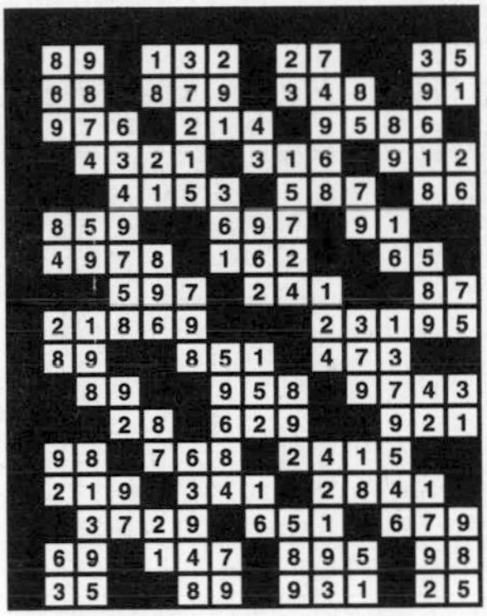

Puzzle 203

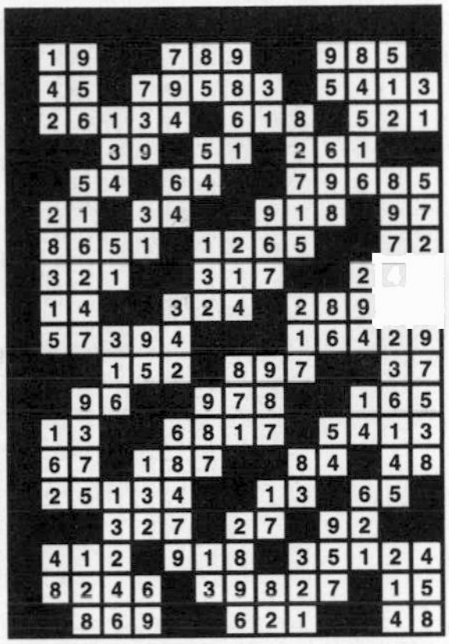

Puzzle 204

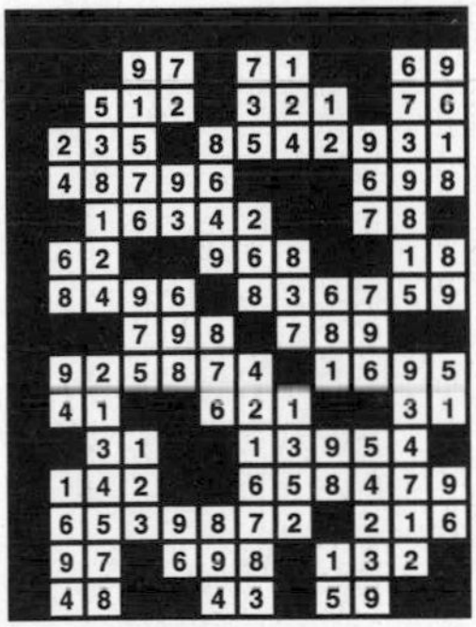

Puzzle 205

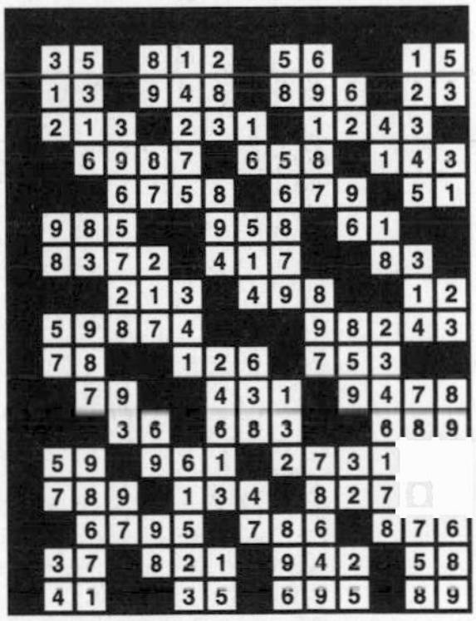

Puzzle 206

Puzzle 207

Puzzle 208

Puzzle 209

Puzzle 210

Puzzle 211

Puzzle 212

Puzzle 213

Puzzle 214

Puzzle 215

Puzzle 216

Puzzle 217

Puzzle 218

Puzzle 219

Puzzle 220

Puzzle 221

Puzzle 222

Puzzle 223

Puzzle 224

Puzzle 225

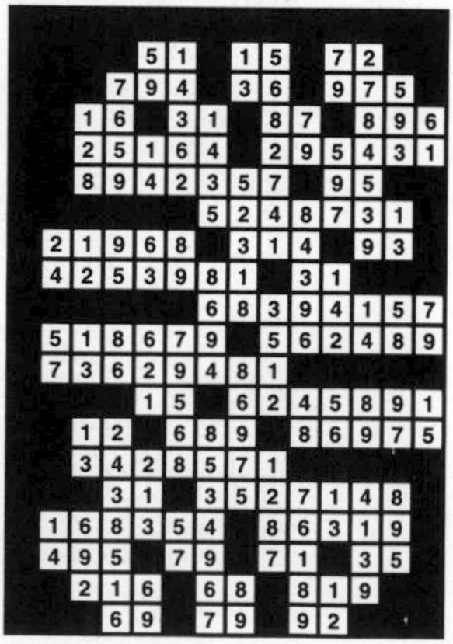

Puzzle 226

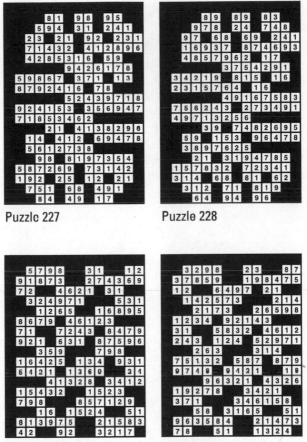

Puzzle 227

Puzzle 228

Puzzle 229

Puzzle 230

Puzzle 231

Diabolically Difficult

Puzzle 232

Puzzle 233

Puzzle 234

Puzzle 235

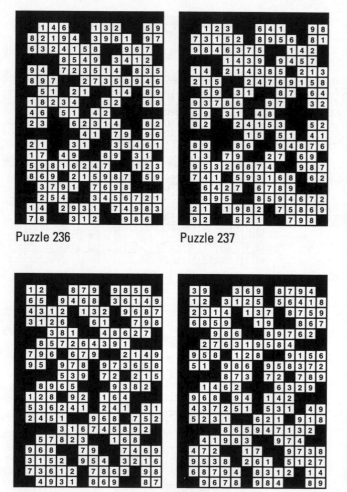

Puzzle 236

Puzzle 237

Puzzle 238

Puzzle 239

Puzzle 240

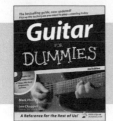

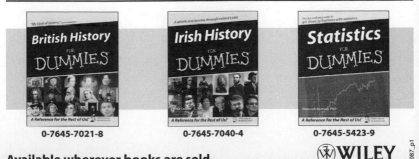